RAINFOREST SAFARI

The Five Mile Press Pty Ltd
1 Centre Road, Scoresby
Victoria 3179 Australia
Email: publishing@fivemile.com.au
Website: www.fivemile.com.au

First published 2008
This edition published in 2008 by The Five Mile Press Pty Ltd

Printed in China 5 4 3 2 1

Project Editor: Gareth Jones
Copy Editor: Liz Dittner
Senior Art Editor: Gülen Shevki-Taylor
Designer: Emma Wicks
Picture Research: Steve Behan
Production: Lisa Moore; Sophie Martin

ISBN 978 1 74178 503 6

RAINFOREST
SAFARI

JAMES PARRY

FOREWORD BY JOHN BURTON OF THE WORLD LAND TRUST

The Five Mile Press

CONTENTS

OPPOSITE Beireis' Treefrog *Hyla leucophyllata* on orchid *Cattleya guttata*. Like many frogs, this species has various colour morphs, in this instance representing excellent camouflage.

Foreword

James Parry has written a glorious evocation of the beauties of the world's rainforests. I am fortunate enough to have visited these unique ecosystems in many parts of the world, and as CEO of the World Land Trust, I also work for an organisation dedicated to ensuring that some of them, at least, will survive into the future.

Awareness and knowledge are the first steps towards saving these precious ecosystems; if we appreciate the world's rainforests, we are inspired to do something towards conserving them for the future, and this is one reason why I welcome this evocative book.

Unfortunately, almost everywhere, the world's remaining rainforests are under threat. Many have been lost already, and generations to come may never know what their country really looked like, just as many people do not appreciate that the British Isles were once covered with a habitat very similar to the temperate rainforests of the Pacific North-west, or Tasmania. The warm Atlantic winds, laden with moisture deposited their rain on the giant oaks of primeval Britain. All that remains of these towering forests are archaeological remains in the form of timber piles used by the Romans. And later, as Europeans explored and colonized the rest of the world, their demand for timber led to the destruction of the mahogany forests of the Caribbean, and continues to this day, with forests still disappearing at an alarming rate.

And with the Europeans came their technologies, from iron saws, to guns, wheels and ocean-going ships, and later chain saws. All of which contributed to the destruction of the forests and their wildlife. It is all too easy to blame the destruction on Europeans, but once this Pandora's Box of new technologies had been opened, indigenous peoples all over the world were often eager to use them, and they became just as adept at hunting wildlife, or cutting down the forest, though fortunately, not on the industrial scale of the European invaders. However, even now, the slash-and-burn approach of the small-scale farmers is having an increasingly devastating effect on the remaining forests.

By the beginning of the twenty-first century, the massive impacts of the world's burgeoning human population was becoming apparent through climate change, and the role of forests in regulating climate change was generally accepted. However, as I write, it is still true that around 20% of the carbon emissions on the planet come from the destruction of forests and other natural habitats. And while the human population continues to grow, virtually out of control, there is little hope of doing more than stabilizing the rate of destruction of the rainforests of the world. The arguments for conserving rainforests are numerous and diverse; even on strictly utilitarian grounds they are worth saving. But on aesthetic grounds they are an astounding resource. How is it that in the twenty-first century, we humans are prepared to spend billions of pounds, euros, dollars and yen, on an entertainment such as the Olympics, millions on paintings, millions restoring buildings, but not devote a similar fraction of our wealth to irreplaceable nature?

This book revels in the glories and splendour of the rainforests of the world, and I hope after reading it, you will be inspired to join the fight to save what is left.

JOHN BURTON
THE WORLD LAND TRUST

PREVIOUS **Particularly rich in ferns, Daintree National Park in Queensland is one of the most interesting and wildlife-rich rainforest sites in Australia's "Wet Tropics".**

OPPOSITE **A jewel-like male Violet-crowned Woodnymph** *Thalurania colombica*, **photographed in Costa Rica. Found only in the Americas, there are over 320 species of hummingbird, many of which live in rainforests.**

Introduction

Rainforests are the greatest natural show on Earth, yet their magical qualities may not always be immediately obvious to everyone. I recall a friend regaling me with horror stories following a trip she had made into the Brazilian Amazon – so much rain, heat and oppressive humidity, all day and night, plus clouds of biting insects intent on evading the most pernicious forms of repellent. Slogging through thick vegetation, up to her knees in mud and constantly faced with a barrage of hostile thorns and razor-sharp leaves. And if that were not enough, she exclaimed, there was hardly anything to see: just the occasional monkey (crick in neck required to see those, of course), and a few parrots screeching overhead from time to time. She couldn't wait to get back to Rio.

By their very nature rainforests are certainly wet and lushly vegetated, and it can indeed be hard to spot wildlife up in the dense canopy. But my friend's response had, of course, missed the key point. For while there is no denying that rainforests can be uncomfortable places at times, the rewards they offer are huge – greater, indeed, than any other landscape on the planet. Nowhere else harbours such a wealth of plants and animals, nor represents such a celebration of life. Absorbing the scale of this diversity and beauty requires a little patience and perseverance, until one's senses are "tuned in" to a dimension from which we have become largely disconnected in our everyday lives. For the beauty of the rainforest is in the detail – in the iridescent scales of a butterfly's wing, the glistening waxy slopes inside a pitcher plant, and the subtle murmurings that link the more ear-shattering components of a hidden bird's extravagant song.

Focusing on these seemingly modest aspects of the rainforest does not of course mean that the broad canvas is without impact – there can be few more impressive sights than a sweeping vista of intact primary rainforest. But turning one's attention to the detail helps make the rainforest accessible, containing its scale from the overwhelming to the manageable. It is tempting to conclude that an apprehensive response to the forest might reflect a primeval fear of the wildwood, traditionally regarded in European folklore at least as a place of danger and foreboding. Yet in Africa, Asia, Australasia and South America there are millions of people who for thousands of years have lived quite contentedly within the confines of the rainforest, in perfect harmony and familiarity with an environment that provides for all their needs and of which they have no cause for fear. They are a world away, of course, from a young farmer interviewed recently on British television about what would happen if his land were taken out of crop production and left to go "wild". He was mortified at the prospect: "But nature will take over, and it will become nothing but a useless jungle!" Sadly, it is this latter view that has formed the basis of mankind's overall response to – and exploitation of – rainforests over the last century and more.

The sites chosen for inclusion in this book represent a cross-section of the world's rainforests, their current status a reflection of the ways in which human activity has affected them in recent decades. Some are now mere fragments of their former selves, whereas others remain largely intact. All are important, but almost all are under threat of one sort or another, regardless of protective status. Excellent conservation work is already making a difference in many of these places but how to ensure the survival of the rainforests, and of the wildlife they support, remains one of the most pressing environmental issues facing us today.

JAMES PARRY

LEFT **Hornbills are classic inhabitants of the South-east Asian rainforests, and hard to miss. These are Knobbed Hornbills *Aceros cassidix* from Sulawesi, with the male in the foreground and female behind.**

Rainforests: Context and Characteristics

Despite covering only seven per cent or so of the Earth's land surface, rainforests are already known to contain more than half of the planet's scientifically described species. There may be as many as 30 million different types of flora and fauna living in rainforest habitats and, with rainforest ecology still in its infancy, our understanding of their requirements and of how these ecosystems function remains largely incomplete. Such remarkable abundance is a result of the convergence of all the ingredients required for life to flourish in particular exuberance. It is also a reflection of the vast range of discrete ecological niches that have evolved under the immense rainforest umbrella.

It is a truism, but rainforests are essentially about rain, and lots of it. Precise definitions vary, but an annual rainfall total in excess of 1,800 millimetres (70 inches) or thereabouts is generally considered necessary to sustain the lush vegetation that is characteristic of a rainforest. Although this principle can be applied universally, it is really the only firm-and-fast rule with rainforests; the other criteria that help define and explain the different types are much less clear-cut and are subject to differing climatic, regional and topographical factors. Even within the rainfall "requirement" there are important variations; in regions where rainfall is spread relatively evenly through the year, rainforests are overwhelmingly evergreen in character. But elsewhere, rainfall – whilst copious in total quantity – may be for the most part restricted to particular times of year, with a defined dry season or seasons. In these rainforests many of the trees may be deciduous, shedding their foliage during the drier months and coming into leaf at the beginning of the rainy season. These are often termed "monsoon forests", and occur typically in south-west India.

Temperature and sunlight are also critical elements in the rainforest environment, but their character and implications can vary greatly between different types of rainforest. High average temperatures in the range of 25–30°C (77–86°F) are typical of the classic equatorial lowland rainforests found across the Amazon and Congo Basins, for example. Yet in the forests of maritime western North America, which in terms of rainfall and vegetation are just as much rainforests as those found in the equatorial zone, mean temperatures are much cooler, averaging 6–15°C (43–59°F). However, the key element shared by these

BELOW The vegetation in temperate rainforests, such as here in Mount Field National Park in Tasmania, Australia, is easily as luxuriant as in their equatorial counterparts. Definitions of rainforest vary, but most authorities agree that the Atlantic oakwoods of the western British Isles, for example, qualify as temperate rainforests.

RIGHT **Mandrills live in the rainforests of West-central Africa. The dramatic facial markings of the male are one of the more obvious aspects of sexual selection and become more vivid in colour when he is aroused.**

LEFT Found in the montane rainforests of Central America, the Resplendent Quetzal *Pharomachrus mocinno* is one of the most extravagantly plumaged of all forest birds. Its iridescent feathers were highly prized among the Aztecs for ceremonial use.

two types of rainforest (other than similarly high levels of rainfall) is a climate in which temperatures are predominantly equable all year round, with no pronounced extremes, either diurnal or seasonal.

The impact of sunlight also varies considerably in the rainforest environment. Tropical regions, with roughly 12 hours of daylight throughout the year, receive at least twice as much solar radiation as do the polar regions, for example, and so plant growth is prolific and fairly constant throughout the year. Yet in equatorial montane rainforests, i.e. those above 1,000 metres (3,300 feet) in altitude, sunshine levels are often considerably reduced owing to a greater degree of cloud cover and a high incidence of mist and fog. In the so-called cloudforests (the dominant tropical ecosystem between 2,000 and 3,500 metres/6,000–11,500 feet or so) the lower sunlight totals mean that photosynthesis rates are greatly compromised and so plant growth is much slower than in lowland rainforests. Yet, although lowland rainforest may claim greater diversity and higher numbers of plant species, cloudforest vegetation can be equally luxuriant and groups such as bamboos, ferns and bromeliads are particularly well represented. However, trees and shrubs in this environment tend to be of more modest stature than their lowland counterparts, and at very high altitudes the vegetation is particularly restricted in size and appropriately termed "elfin woodland" – but still regarded as a type of rainforest.

Even at sunnier lower altitudes, only 1–3 per cent of the sunlight that hits the upper tree canopy actually penetrates the thick layers of vegetation and reaches the forest floor. As a result, in mature primary rainforest with a well-developed canopy there can be relatively little understorey vegetation. One obvious characteristic of such forests is the presence of emergents, huge trees that rise above the main canopy, often to a height of 60 metres (200 feet) or more. Many such trees have the massive buttress roots that are an integral part of the rainforest scene. Average canopy heights vary, but are mostly between 30 and 40 metres (100–130 feet). The structure of a rainforest is largely dictated by the constant quest for light; when a large tree falls and light floods into the resulting gap, a race is immediately underway to fill it. So-called pioneer species, their seeds lying dormant in the forest floor soil awaiting an opportunity to burst into growth, quickly germinate and grow rapidly. In the case of species of *Cecropia*, one of the most common "gap"-colonizing plant groups in the neotropics, the rate of growth can be as much as 2.5 metres (8 feet 2 inches) per annum.

In terms of overall vegetation, rainforests are clearly notable for the vast number of tree species they support. In particularly rich forests more than 400 species have been recorded from 1 hectare (2.5 acres), a remarkable level of diversity. However, the majority of the biomass (i.e. the total weight of living organisms) in tropical rainforests may well be accounted for by the vines, lianas and the immense variety of epiphytes that festoon the trees. Epiphytes are not parasitic – they simply lodge on other plants, benefiting from the conditions and habitat niches they offer. Ferns, orchids and bromeliads are the most obvious in tropical forests, while in temperate rainforests the profusion of ferns is accompanied by plentiful mosses, lichens and lungworts. Although temperate rainforests are less biodiverse than those in the tropics, they hold their own – at least – in terms of biomass, and their trees regularly exceed equatorial forest species in terms of height and trunk girth.

Tropical rainforests are also characterized by an abundance of palm species, a group that can be especially prominent in association with mangrove forests. These are a particularly important type of lowland rainforest found along shallow coasts, estuaries and tidal rivers in the tropical zone, where they are a vital element of the coastal ecosystem. Palms are also often well represented in swamp forests and in the seasonally flooded forests of the Amazon, where conditions are so extreme that plants have evolved special adaptations to ensure their survival. Fish play an important role as seed dispersal agents in these flooded forests, and some tree species have evolved pulpy seedcases, which keep the seeds afloat when they drop from the tree into the water. They are then eaten by fish and thereby dispersed elsewhere within the flooded network – a classic example of the extraordinary complexity and symbiotic character of the rainforest environment.

BELOW **One of the world's largest butterflies, Rajah Brooke's Birdwing** *Trogonoptera brookiana* **is found in Peninsular Malaysia, Borneo and Sumatra. Although still relatively common in some areas, rainforest destruction and illegal collection are having an impact on its numbers.**

Map of Locations

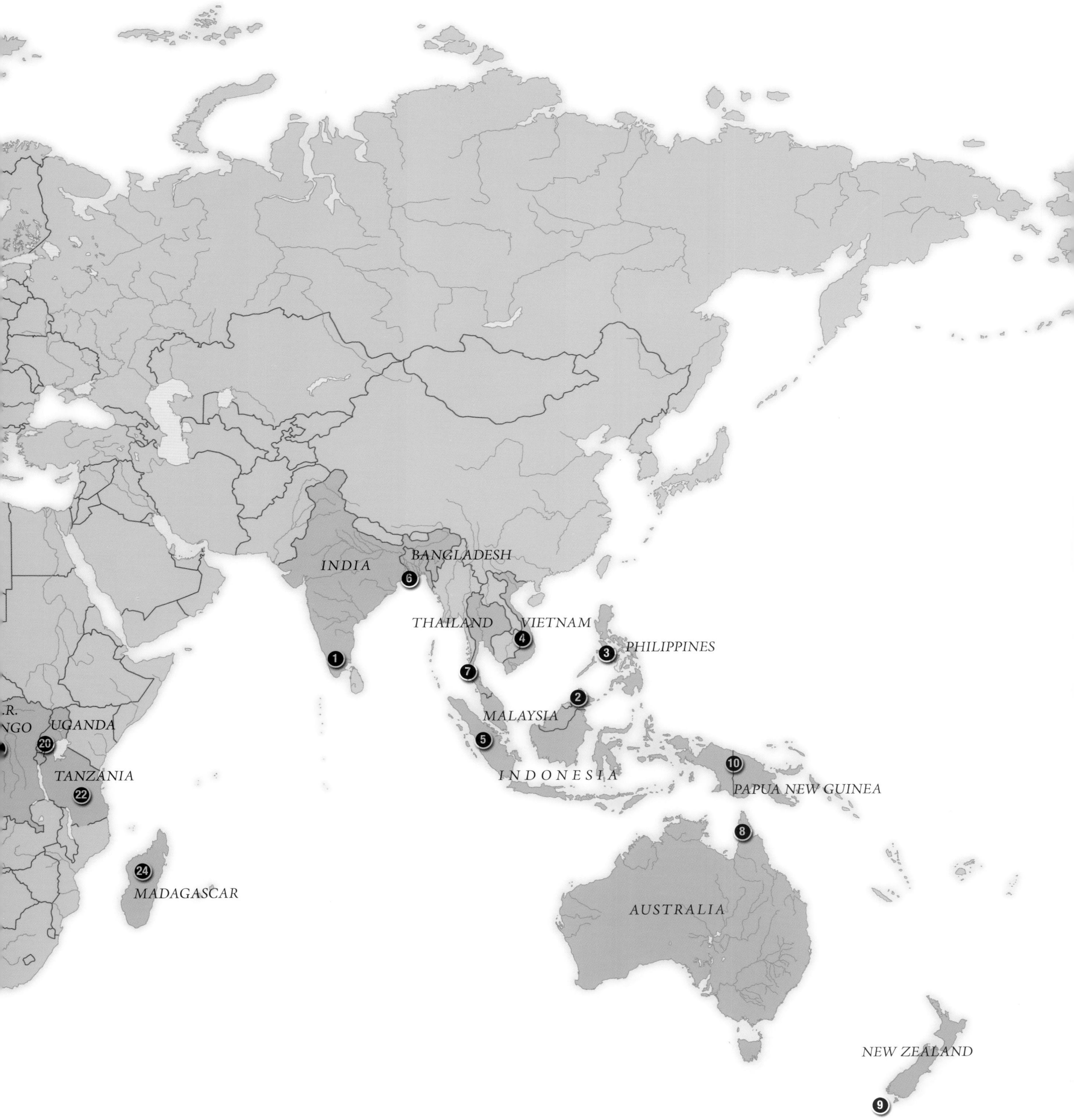

.R.
NGO
UGANDA
20
TANZANIA
22
24
MADAGASCAR
INDIA
6
BANGLADESH
1
THAILAND
7
VIETNAM
4
PHILIPPINES
3
2
MALAYSIA
5
INDONESIA
10
PAPUA NEW GUINEA
8
AUSTRALIA
NEW ZEALAND
9

ASIA

Rainforest is the dominant vegetation type across much of tropical Asia, from parts of India east to Vietnam, southern China and the islands around the South China Sea. Until the late-nineteenth century much of this forest was relatively intact, but it has been seriously degraded and fragmented since then by extensive logging, infrastructural development and agricultural expansion. The recent impacts of deforestation on parts of Indonesia and Malaysia are well known, but sizeable tracts of undisturbed primary rainforest still survive in southern Asia, often in upland areas where human access is more difficult. Some of these rank among the world's most important biodiversity hotspots and continue to harbour a great variety of wildlife, including fast-declining populations of large mammals such as Asian Elephant and Tiger. A further important aspect of Asian rainforests is their wide variety, ranging from the classic lowland vegetation of Borneo to the montane rainforests of Vietnam and the dense mangrove tracts of the Sundarbans in Bangladesh and India.

LEFT The Sumatran Tiger *Panthera tigris sumatrae* is the smallest Tiger subspecies and critically endangered. Fewer than 400 individuals are estimated to survive in the rainforests of Sumatra and the number is falling.

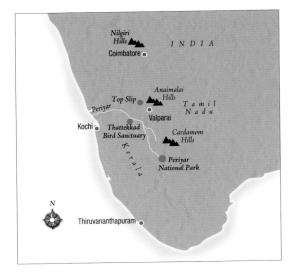

1. The Remnant Rainforests of the Southern Ghats, India

Extending for some 1,600 kilometres (almost 995 miles) along the western coast of India northwards from its southern tip, the Western Ghat mountains contain some of that country's greatest landscapes and most interesting wildlife areas. This is the second-highest mountain chain in the subcontinent after the Himalayas, and runs in a continuous chain except for one main interruption, the Palghat Gap, 30 kilometres (19 miles) wide. The uplands south of this break are usually referred to as the Southern Ghats, and together with those to the north serve to intercept the south-west monsoon, soaking up most of the precipitation and thereby dictating the rainfall regime of much of the rest of Peninsular India.

With their steep west-facing slopes subject to annual rain totals of up to 2,500 millimetres (100 inches), 80 per cent of which falls during June to September, the Western/Southern Ghats also serve as the main watershed for southern India, feeding networks of rivers that run to both the west and the east. The chain's complicated topography is responsible for the diverse range of indigenous vegetation types found here, from tropical lowland rainforest to montane elfin woodland and high-altitude grassland, an array of habitat niches supporting high levels of endemic flora and fauna. The Ghats are one of the world's top biodiversity hotspots; some 5,000 vascular plants have been recorded here, of which 1,700 or so are endemic. Among vertebrates, the highest rates of endemism occur among reptiles and amphibians, two-thirds of which are found only here, but there are also 16 species of endemic bird (almost all of which are forest species) and up to 20 endemic mammals, although further research into less well-understood groups such as bats and rodents may see this total grow even further.

Since the early twentieth century the forest cover of the Ghats has been reduced from approximately 160,000 square kilometres (62,000 square miles) to just 13,000 (5,000). The area between the mountains and the Indian Ocean, for example, traditionally known as the Malabar Coast, was originally covered with lush, tropical semi-evergreen and deciduous rainforest, but very little closed-canopy forest remains here today. This is one of the most densely populated parts of India, and intensively farmed. Much of the indigenous forest was cleared to make way for agricultural

RIGHT The Malabar Parakeet is endemic to the Western Ghats and fairly common within its restricted range. Gaudy plumage and noisy calls make these birds difficult to miss, especially when massed on fruiting trees.

OPPOSITE An isolated stand of secondary forest amid tea plantations near Valparai. In the distance relatively intact *shola* forest extends up the mountain slopes. In the foreground what was once a permanent forest stream survives only as a seasonal watercourse, evidence of the impact deforestation can have on watersheds.

land, or selectively logged and interplanted with commercial tree species such as teak. When left to develop naturally, as some now are, such sites can be important for wildlife. For example, the area now protected by the Thattekkad Bird Sanctuary, on the banks of the Periyar River, was described by the renowned Indian ornithologist Dr Salim Ali as being "the richest bird habitat in Peninsular India" in the 1930s. Much of the forest here was later felled and sectors converted to teak or rubber production, but with the forest now regenerating, the sanctuary's 25 square kilometres (9.5 square miles) remain an outstanding site for birdlife. Some 270 different species have been recorded here.

Many of the region's avian endemics are present at Thattekkad, including Malabar Grey Hornbill *Ocyceros griseus*, Malabar Parakeet *Psittacula columboides* and White-bellied Treepie *Dendrocitta leucogastra*, all of which are relatively easy to see. The sanctuary is also home to the rather more secretive Malabar Trogon *Harpactes fasciatus*, undoubtedly among the most stunning of all Indian birds but not always straightforward to locate as it sits motionless in the canopy. A wide range of waterbirds lives in the riverine scrub, including several species of kingfisher, and the whole sanctuary is good for owls. Other wildlife includes Asian Elephant *Elephas maximus*, herds of which move regularly through the area and congregate particularly near the river, as well as highly peripatetic packs of Wild Dog or Dhole *Cuon alpinus* and even the very occasional Tiger *Panthera tigris*.

Interesting tracts of remnant habitat near Thattekkad include the mixed evergreen/moist deciduous forest at Urulanthanni. This area still retains a good number of mature trees, with characteristic species including *Xylia xylocarpa*, renowned for its durable and termite-resistant wood, *Tetrameles nudiflora*, unmistakable with its massive wall-like buttresses, and the elegant *Haldina cordifolia*, noted for a straight, clean bole which can be branchless to a height of 20 metres (65 feet) or more. This forest is a good site for the endemic Malabar Giant Squirrel *Ratufa indica*, as well as for one of the most bizarre of nocturnal birds, the Sri Lanka Frogmouth *Batrachostomus moniliger*, best looked for at its daytime roosts just a couple of metres above the ground.

ABOVE **The Western Ghats support India's largest population of wild Asian Elephant. Several thousand live here, one of the best places to observe them being Periyar National Park, although herds wander widely across the region.**

ABOVE Another Western Ghats endemic, the Malabar Grey Hornbill is often heard before it is seen. Its raucous, slightly deranged-sounding call is a common sound in the lowland rainforest.

RIGHT Riparian forest along the Periyar River at Thattekkad. This habitat is rich in birdlife and best explored by boat along the river. In the evenings elephants sometimes come to drink, but are generally very wary and surprisingly difficult to see well.

OPPOSITE TOP **A forest track at Urulanthanni. The undisturbed nature of this area of forest makes it an excellent site for wildlife, but this quality may be affected by proposals to upgrade the road and make it suitable for lorries and trucks.**

OPPOSITE BOTTOM **The Malabar Giant Squirrel is a characteristic species of the Ghats forests. Variable in coloration, it is very much an inhabitant of the canopy and only rarely leaves the safety of tall trees. It can reach a length of over 1 metre (3 feet), more than half of which is tail.**

In forests like Urulanthanni the transition is quite distinct from evergreen forest through moist deciduous to dry deciduous, the presence of high humidity indicators such as lianas becoming noticeably less as the habitat becomes drier. The range of vegetation types here also includes thick stands of bamboo, the haunt of the increasingly scarce Slender Loris *Loris tardigradus* and of one of the world's blue riband reptiles, the King Cobra *Ophiophagus hannah*. The world's longest venomous snake, King Cobras have a fearsome reputation (large specimens can exceed 5.5 metres/18 feet and their venom can overpower an adult human in seconds). Yet like most snakes, they will always try to avoid contact with humans and rarely attack unless in self defence, and only then after a sustained threat display. Inhabitants of dense forest, they are particularly partial to streamside thickets, where the female makes a ground nest of leaves and dead vegetation in which to incubate her eggs. Any exploration of such habitat must therefore be undertaken with the utmost care!

The decimation of the region's lowland forests was mirrored by similar destruction at higher elevations, with an onslaught on the montane rainforests that occur above 1,000 metres (3,300 feet) or so. In the Anaimalai hills, for example, which contain southern India's highest mountain, Anai Mudi (2,695 metres/8,842 feet), extensive tracts of forest were destroyed from the late nineteenth century onwards. Once all potentially valuable timber was extracted, the remaining vegetation was totally cleared to make way for plantations of tea, coffee, cashew and cardamom, as well as introduced commercial tree species such as eucalyptus, which were used as fuel in the tea-production process. This pattern of land use was replicated elsewhere in the Western Ghats, such as in the Nilgiri Hills, the source of what is reputedly the best tea in India.

The name Anaimalai comes from the Tamil words for "elephant" and "mountain", and up to the mid-nineteenth century this area was renowned among sportsmen for the game that thrived there. This included large herds of elephant and Gaur *Bos gaurus*, as well as good numbers of both Tiger *Panthera tigris* and Leopard *P. pardus*, but much of the wildlife was later displaced, or disappeared entirely in the face of the expanding plantation monoculture. However, limited areas of primary forest did survive, and some of the best examples are now safeguarded within three adjoining

BELOW **King Cobras are very much at home in water, and show a distinct liking for streamside vegetation. They feed mainly on other snakes, but will also take lizards, small mammals and eggs.**

areas on the Kerala/Tamil Nadu state border: the Anaimalai or Indira Gandhi National Park (more popularly known as "Top Slip", the name given to the site here from where felled timber was traditionally slid down the steep slopes – the easiest way of getting it to the bottom), Parambikulam Wildlife Sanctuary and Eravikulum National Park. The latter is famous for its population of Nilgiri Tahr *Nilgiritragus hylocrius*, an endemic species of wild goat that lives on the high grassland slopes. Typical of the higher elevations, such as on the Hamilton Plateau, are the dense thickets of evergreen montane rainforest, known as *shola*, which are interspersed with grassland in a characteristic mosaic.

Despite the disappearance of large areas of native forest, the adaptability – or perhaps simple persistence – of certain types of animal means that some of the best wildlife watching is to be had in the remnant patches of forest scattered across the agro-industrial landscape of tea plantations. Around the town of Valparai, for example, there is no remaining primary forest, just a few mature trees that were spared the axe and have survived in the gardens of tea planters' residences. However, there are extensive fragments of regenerating secondary forest, and these can be good places in which to seek out the two local endemic primates, Lion-tailed Macaque *Macaca silenus* and Nilgiri Langur *Trachypithecus johnii*, as well as small numbers of Gaur and the skulking Indian Muntjac or Barking Deer *Muntiacus muntjak*.

Among predators, Leopards are not uncommon here but rarely give even the briefest of views, their presence usually revealed only by the agitated alarm cries of macaques or langurs. Even Tigers are occasionally seen, moving through the plantations between patches of forest. These are usually young adult males, forced to leave their natal area by their mother and seek a territory of their

ABOVE **The highly distinctive Lion-tailed Macaque survives across the Western Ghats in patches of secondary forest. Although primarily arboreal, troops will descend to ground level to forage for fallen fruit and other food items.**

RIGHT The handsome Malabar Trogon (this is a male bird) is widely distributed in forest areas of southern India. Finding one can be tricky, as they have a habit of sitting motionless on a branch for long periods before suddenly flying away through the trees at high speed.

RIGHT The Malabar Whistling-thrush *Myophonus horsfieldii* is a bird of dense forest and scrub, often found near water and in the vicinity of rocks. Its distinctive whistling song is a characteristic sound of the Western Ghats.

own. They are therefore often pushed into marginal areas such as this, making them vulnerable to poachers and bringing them into what are often potentially dangerous confrontations with humans. A more common source of strife locally are wild elephants, several thousand of which live in the Western Ghats. With many of their traditional seasonal migration routes now blocked by human changes to the landscape and habitat, the elephants are increasingly confined to smaller areas. At certain times of year around Valparai small groups are regularly seen moving through the tea plantations and forest fragments, poignantly following ancestral routes across a landscape now largely unsuitable for them. This can bring them into conflict with humans, especially when they raid crops – there have even been instances of them entering houses in search of food.

Living with large animals such as elephants is never easy, least of all in a country with a burgeoning human population and currently enjoying rapid economic growth. Infrastructural developments such as road-building, dam construction and irrigation schemes can all spell disaster for already fragile habitats and their associated wildlife. As human density around protected areas has grown, so illegal encroachment has become a major issue across the region (and, indeed, the whole country). Meanwhile, the devolution of power away from central government in Delhi to provincial level has, in the eyes of many Indian conservationists, adversely affected their cause. Bureaucracy, corruption and internal wrangling are hampering many aspects of wildlife and habitat protection, including within the network of protected areas. Some optimism for the future is however offered through the development of ecotourism in locations like Valparai, for example, where homestays in ex-colonial bungalows and wildlife-viewing led by local guides offer the critical advantage of engaging local people through making wildlife conservation work for them economically.

BELOW **Extensive tracts of forest survive in protected areas of the Western Ghats, but more conservation effort is required to ensure connectivity between them. This will allow the continued movement of large mammals such as elephants.**

RIGHT **The dramatic White-bellied Treepie is a target species for most visiting birders to south-west India. A reasonably common species, it prefers evergreen habitats and does well in secondary growth forest.**

SOUTH CHINA SEA

N

MALAYSIA

BRUNEI

Sepilok Orang-utan
Sanctuary

Kota Kinabalu
Sandakan
Lahad Datu

Danum Valley
Conservation Area

Sarawak

Kuching

Kalimantan

INDONESIA

2. The Orang-utans of Borneo's Danum Valley

Few animals are as appealing to human eyes and sentiment as Orang-utans. Their proximity to us genetically – they may share over 96 per cent of their genes with *Homo sapiens* – doubtless helps explain the fascination they hold for us, many of their physical characteristics and behavioural aspects being so recognizably akin to our own that we cannot fail to feel a connection. Furthermore, the plight of Orang-utans in recent years, with numbers declining fast as their rainforest home is cut down, burned and converted to commercial plantations, has made their predicament all the more poignant in a world increasingly horrified at the environmental destruction taking place. Orang-utans have come to symbolize the fate of the rainforests in which they live and on which they depend.

This engaging animal occurs only on the islands of Borneo and Sumatra, with the populations on each island recognized as separate species, *Pongo pygmaeus* and *Pongo abelii* respectively. The Bornean species is itself divided into three geographically demarcated sub-species. Populations of Orangs on both islands have fallen dramatically in recent decades in the wake of the widespread rainforest destruction that has taken place across the region. The most recent available estimates

RIGHT The playful and engaging nature of Orang-utans has helped put them right at the top of the conservation agenda. Habitat destruction and the activities of the illegal pet trade have seen numbers fall considerably, and the species is now extinct in substantial areas of its former range.

OPPOSITE The lush rainforest of the Danum Valley is one of the most biodiverse places in Asia and a reminder of the wildlife-rich habitat that was once found much more widely across the south-eastern parts of the continent.

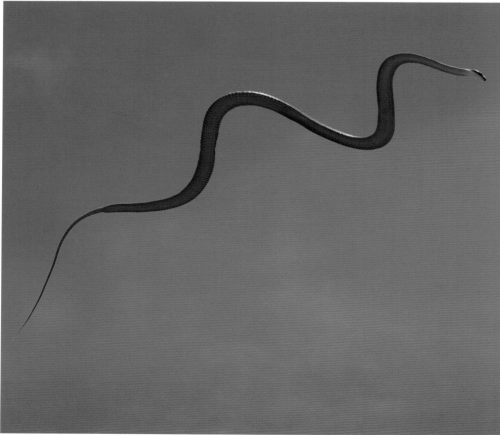

ABOVE AND LEFT **Borneo's 'flying snakes'** are the stuff of legend. There are two species (this is the Paradise Flying Snake *Chrysopelea paradisi*), but neither truly flies. Instead, they glide, launching themselves out of the tree canopy and flattening out their bodies to create air resistance so that a gliding descent is possible. They can even exert some control over the direction of the glide by moving their bodies from side to side as they descend.

(2004) put the Bornean population at approximately 15,300 and the Sumatran at about 7,500; reasonable numbers, on the face of it, but these figures may have been overgenerous at the time and the downward trend has certainly continued since then. Indeed, it is the rapid rate of decline that is the main cause for concern.

On Borneo, Orang-utans survive in increasingly fragmented populations scattered across Kalimantan and Sabah, as well as in parts of Sarawak. They are rather fastidious in terms of the types of rainforest they favour, showing a distinct preference for freshwater swamp forest, where adequate and reliable water levels help ensure a year-round supply of fruiting trees, and for "extreme" lowland dipterocarp forest, i.e. that below 150 metres (490 feet) above sea level. They also occur at lower densities in other types of forest and at higher altitudes, although montane rainforest is almost always avoided.

One of the main Orang "hotspots" in Borneo is the Danum Valley Conservation Area (DVCA) in eastern Sabah, covering 438 square kilometres (169 square miles) of some of the best surviving undisturbed dipterocarp rainforest on the whole island. Formerly part of a logging concession, this area was specifically spared the fate of many other such forests in Borneo on account of its very high levels of biodiversity and high conservation value. The forest here is dominated by dipterocarps such as *Parashorea malaanonan*, *P. tomentella* and *Shorea johorensis* and supports many of the classic wildlife species of South-east Asian rainforests, albeit in relict populations now largely cut off from those elsewhere on the island. Over 340 species of bird have been recorded here, including all seven of the hornbill species found in Borneo, as well as some 120 mammal species and an impressive variety of reptiles and amphibians. There is probably no other place in Borneo to match it.

The undisturbed nature of the forest in DVCA, thanks largely to a traditionally light human presence and little incidence of illegal hunting, has helped ensure the continued presence of large

ABOVE Thick vegetation does not make for easy wildlife watching. Spotting animals and birds is often easier along watercourses or where clearings allow better visibility. Open gaps in the forest also provide opportunities for so-called pioneer plant species, which grow in response to the greater light levels.

RIGHT **Borneo is outstanding for orchids, with approximately 1,500 species already described and doubtless others awaiting scientific discovery. A widespread rainforest species is *Dendrobium secundum*, sometimes known as the Toothbrush Orchid.**

OPPOSITE **The extraordinary Tarsier is seen quite often at Danum, usually by torchlight on special nocturnal walks, when visitors are taken out to experience the rainforest at night. Daytime views are very rare.**

mammals such as Asian Elephant, here present in its diminutive Bornean race, *Elephas maximus borneensis*, Banteng *Bos javanicus* and the critically endangered Sumatran Rhinoceros *Dicerorhinus sumatrensis*. This is also one of the best places in the world to try and see Western Tarsier *Tarsius bancanus*, a bizarre nocturnal primate, only 13 centimetres (5 inches) or so long, with frog-like feet and huge staring eyes that give off a pale pink reflection in torchlight. However, it is in the hope of watching wild Orangs that many visitors come to Danum. Together with the Ulu Segama Malua Forest Reserves, which cover 2,400 square kilometres (925 square miles) adjacent to the DVCA, the area is home to the largest surviving population of Orang-utans in Malaysian Borneo. Possibly as many as 4,000 individuals live here, their presence a major reason behind the 2006 decision by the state government of Sabah to phase out logging activity in these forest reserves.

Although there is a healthy population of Orangs in the DVCA, actually seeing them is another matter. Wild Orangs are shy animals and, unlike other great apes (and, indeed, primates generally), they are rather solitary by nature. Finding one as it moves around high in the canopy while searching for food, often surprisingly discreetly, can be a matter of luck as much as anything. However, experienced local guides usually have a good idea whether Orangs are present in any particular area of forest and where they may have made their overnight "nests". On occasion these have even been constructed adjacent to the canopy walkway that has been built at Danum to give an eye-to-eye view of life in the canopy, almost 30 metres (100 feet) above the forest floor.

Checking out fruiting trees is always worthwhile, as Orangs are mainly frugivorous and will readily congregate where fruit is plentiful, often remaining there until the supply is exhausted. Evidence suggests that every wild Orang-utan maintains a "mental map" of the main sources of fruit within its home range, with information logged in terms of the precise location of particular trees, when they last fruited, the distance between them, etc. In this way intelligence and simple reasoning

Two young orphan Orangs, photographed at Sepilok Orang-utan Sanctuary. The sad plight of such individuals has helped raise global awareness of what can be a lengthy rehabilitation process and one that cannot always result in the release of the animals back into the wild.

help an Orang-utan survive most effectively in the rainforest environment. Although they have defined home ranges, Orangs are not usually territorial in a defensive sense and will often overlap with one another, peaceably sharing a particular area of forest with several others of the same species. Only when two mature males come face to face is any sort of altercation likely.

In recent years the plight of Orang-utans has been the focus of frequent media attention. Although strong laws exist on paper protecting them and specifically prohibiting their harming and capture, in reality this legislation is wantonly flouted. Wild Orangs are still killed illegally by loggers, and young animals continue to be taken for animal "shows" and circuses, as well as for the illicit pet trade. Evidence suggests that the latter at least may be less prevalent than during its heyday in the 1980s and '90s when, for example, in a five-year period, as many as a thousand baby Orangs were smuggled out of Kalimantan to Taiwan for sale as exotic pets, following a popular Taiwanese television programme that featured an Orang-utan as a pet. In many such cases the mother was undoubtedly slaughtered so that the baby could be taken. Meanwhile, with their natural habitat fast disappearing, wild Orangs are often forced out of the forest in search of food and thereby into close, and often dangerous, contact with humans.

The number of orphaned young Orangs, along with older injured or disoriented animals, is now so high that the Orang-utan orphanages and welfare centres in both Malaysia and Indonesia are struggling to cope. Rehabilitation centres, such as the famous one at Sepilok in Sabah, the first of its type, are aimed at caring for vulnerable Orangs. These are mostly youngsters rescued from unsuitable or illegal captive conditions, and the centres work to equip them with the skills required for their future survival unaided in the wild. The final stage in this process is the relocation, and post-release monitoring, of animals in suitable areas of protected forest. Equally, in cases where Orang-utans have become marooned in fragments of habitat too small to sustain them beyond the short term, translocation to larger tracts of secure forest is considered.

BELOW Pitcher plants, such as these *Nepenthes* sp., are common at Danum. The rims of the "pitchers" produce nectar, attracting insects which then topple in and are prevented from crawling out by the slippery and waxy inside surfaces. The liquid within the pitcher contains digestive enzymes, which absorb the hapless insects.

ABOVE **Much of Borneo's rainforest has been destroyed, the trees felled and the diverse vegetation cleared away in favour of a plantation monoculture of oil palms, in particular. Orang-utans, along with all other forms of rainforest wildlife, have declined in numbers and their ranges contracted in the face of such devastation.**

Orang-utans have lost approximately 80 per cent of their natural habitat in the last two decades and only a fraction of what remains is protected as effectively as the DVCA. Their numbers are continuing to fall, but the outlook need not necessarily be bleak. This is a surprisingly flexible species, able to survive in secondary forest and, indeed, in wood production forests, so long as there is a diversity of appropriate tree and plant species to sustain it. In addition to the benefits of enhanced protection for those forests retaining healthy Orang populations, there is also hope for the future of the species through the rehabilitation of degraded forests. Although many of these have been selectively logged, they can be restored to suitable habitat through the infill planting of fast-growing native tree species. This arrangement can permit the sustainable harvesting of wood products as well as provide a home for Orang-utans and other forest wildlife. And while it is clear that Orangs (and much other wildlife, for that matter) cannot survive in the palm oil plantations that have replaced large areas of rainforest in Borneo in recent years, it should be possible to ensure the survival of the species through the effective protection and management of those remaining natural forests still harbouring viable populations of this magnificent ape.

OPPOSITE **Mimicry is a central component of successful camouflage. This leaf insect *Phyllium* sp. relies on its uncannily leaf-like shape and coloration to escape detection. Such techniques are one reason why the close examination of vegetation is always worthwhile.**

3. The Last Rainforests of the Philippines

An archipelago of 7,107 islands, of which only 15 per cent or so are inhabited, the Philippines were once home to some of the world's finest rainforests. At the turn of the twentieth century most of the islands largely retained their indigenous vegetation, supporting a rich diversity of wildlife and at least 3,500 species of tree. Today less than five per cent of the original lowland rainforest remains, mostly shredded into isolated fragments by some of the most rapacious logging seen anywhere in the world. Very little old-growth forest survives outside protected areas, and even within the national parks and reserves illegal logging and the hunting of wildlife are continual problems. High population density and acute levels of poverty ensure that pressure on surviving areas of forest remains intense. A combination of powerful commercial logging concerns and the desperation of small-scale farmers to eke out a living, usually via short-term shifting cultivation, has been catastrophic for the country's forests and, indeed, for its wider environment.

Miraculously, however, some vestiges of rainforest do survive and conservationists are engaged in a race against time to compile data on what these habitats support and devise strategies aimed at helping ensure their protection. Fieldwork and research continue to confirm the Philippines as one of the world's most important biodiversity hotspots. Most of the islands rose out of the sea and so have never been in contact with a major landmass, their flora and fauna therefore evolving largely in isolation. As a result, levels of endemism in the Philippines are very high. Forty-five per cent of the country's bird species are endemic, for example, with even higher figures for mammals and reptiles/amphibians – 67 and 75 per cent, respectively. Remarkably little is known about many of these species, but what is clear is that many are in serious decline and some are at imminent risk of extinction.

OPPOSITE **One of Asia's largest birds of prey, the Philippine Eagle is the country's national bird. After many decades of decline, numbers appear to be stabilizing and high-profile conservation work is in hand to secure its future.**

BELOW **The distinctive so-called Chocolate Hills on Bohol are a major visitor attraction, but the island is also important for the tracts of rainforest that survive around the hills. These forests support important populations of the endemic Philippine Tarsier *Tarsius syrichta*.**

The understorey of the Philippine rainforest is typically lush, with many ferns and palms. In habitat terms rainforests can usefully be regarded as arranged in vertical strata, with particular creatures occupying niches at certain levels and rarely moving up or down. Many species spend their entire lives in the understorey.

Tropical rainforest is the natural climax vegetation of the lowland Philippines. On the largest island of Luzon one of the most interesting areas of rainforest is within the Subic–Bataan Natural Park, located to the north-west of Manila and one of 10 priority protected areas established across the country in the 1990s following a nationwide ban on logging. The park comprises the Bataan Natural Park and the Subic Watershed Forest Reserve, the latter located within the perimeter of what was, until its closure in 1992, the American naval base of Subic Bay. The forest here was deliberately protected during this period, both for use in jungle survival training and as a security barrier, and it now provides a window on how much of the Philippines would have looked before the destruction of its forests began in earnest during the twentieth century.

Mature primary forest, containing huge dipterocarps (of which some 40 species are found in the Philippines), covers the rolling hills here and extends right down to coast, where extensive tracts of mangrove – a type of vegetation extensively destroyed or damaged elsewhere in the Philippines – still survive. Forest birdlife is abundant and features local specialities such as Luzon Bleeding-heart Pigeon *Gallicolumba luzonica* and Luzon Hornbill *Penelopides manillae*. Mammals include good numbers of Long-tailed Macaque *Macaca fascicularis* and fruit bats, including the endangered Golden-crowned Flying Fox *Acerodon jubatus*.

The remnant forests of Luzon, notably those in the Northern Sierra Madre Natural Park (the country's largest protected area of primary rainforest), are also home to the Philippines' most iconic bird – the Philippine Eagle *Pithecophaga jefferyi*. With a wingspan of 2 metres (6.5 feet), this is one of the world's largest birds of prey and, in the absence of any large predatory mammals, the islands' top predator. Once more widespread, the eagle is now restricted to Luzon, Samar, Leyte and Mindanao, and although no firm figures exist on current population levels, the total number of pairs is estimated at fewer than 150. However, this was probably never a common bird, not least because a breeding pair requires a territory of some 60–100 square kilometres (25–40 square

OPPOSITE TOP Formerly known as the Monkey-eating Eagle, the Philippine Eagle has an immensely powerful beak. Although it will prey on monkeys when available, more usual prey includes small tree-dwelling mammals, notably squirrels and colugos (also known as flying lemurs), and birds such as hornbills.

OPPOSITE BOTTOM Thick-billed Green Pigeons *Treron curvirostra* are typical birds of the Philippine rainforest. Unlike some other species, they are able to cope with conditions in secondary forest and so have remained relatively common and widespread.

miles) and will raise only one chick every other year. Birds pair for life, and are site-faithful, making them particularly vulnerable to habitat destruction, as well as to trophy hunters.

A captive breeding and reintroduction programme on Mindanao has had limited success, and the best safeguards of this bird's future will undoubtedly be public education and the effective protection of its wild habitat. Conservation initiatives include various community-based projects, including an "Adopt-a-Nest" scheme, whereby local people are paid money for reporting occupied eagle nests, with further sums payable at each confirmed stage in the breeding process through to the successful fledging of an eaglet. The rainforests of Mindanao, especially those around Mount Apo – at 2,954 metres (9,692 feet) the Philippines' highest mountain – and Mount Kitanglad, offer perhaps the best chance of glimpsing a wild eagle and the most likely focus for a future population expansion of this magnificent raptor.

The destruction of rainforests across sub-tropical Asia has been largely responsible for the rapid decline in the populations of the various species of wild cattle that were once common across the region. One – the Kouprey *Bos sauveli* – has not been seen since the 1980s and is probably extinct, and the numbers of Gaur *Bos gaurus* and Banteng *Bos javanicus* are greatly reduced. In the Philippines this depressing state of affairs is reflected in the fate of one of the world's smallest

ABOVE The diminutive Tamaraw is declining fast and under severe threat. Unusually for wild cattle, this species is largely solitary and in an increasingly fragmented habitat this can make reproduction difficult.

LEFT The dressy Palawan Peacock-pheasant is an inhabitant of the deep rainforest. Although widely distributed across Palawan, its numbers are declining due to habitat loss and hunting.

species of wild bovid, the Tamaraw *Bubalus mindorensis*. Endemic to the island of Mindoro, and reaching only 110 centimetres (43 inches) at the shoulder, the Tamaraw is the only surviving representative of several species of dwarf buffalo that lived in the Philippines before human colonization of the islands. Many thousands of Tamaraw were once found across Mindoro, but hunting pressure and habitat loss have reduced this population to fewer than 200 individuals. These are largely confined to two areas of fragment rainforest, although they also inhabit the grassland that has replaced the forest. Their future remains uncertain: a captive breeding programme was not successful, and urgent conservation measures are required to prevent the further decline and potential extinction of this intriguing animal.

The islands of Mindoro and Palawan differ from most others in the Philippines in that they were once joined to the Asian mainland. Palawan has a flora and fauna closely related to those found on Borneo, to which it was once connected by a land bridge. This explains the presence here of mammals not found elsewhere in the Philippines, such as porcupines, pangolins and Binturong, with the local form *Arctictis binturong whitei* regarded as an endemic subspecies. Of the 25 non-flying mammals recorded on Palawan archipelago, 11 are endemic and the remaining 14 are shared with Borneo. The birdlife is equally exceptional and includes four endemics, including

the magnificent Palawan Peacock-pheasant *Polyplectron napoleonis*, usually at the top of most visiting birders' wishlists. The island is also one of the last refuges of the Red-vented Corella or Philippine Cockatoo *Cacatua haematuropygia*, once widespread and common across much of the Philippines, but now critically endangered and restricted to a few widely scattered locations. Habitat destruction – it is primarily a bird of lowland rainforest and mangroves – and excessive trapping for the pet trade have been responsible for an alarming crash in numbers.

Its endemic wildlife notwithstanding, Palawan is also important because it retains 50 per cent or so of its original rainforest and also harbours 38 per cent of what remains of the Philippines' once extensive mangrove forests – two of the reasons why the island was declared a biosphere reserve by UNESCO in 1990. Described by one local conservationist as "this country's final forest frontier", Palawan represents a last chance for the Philippines to protect a meaningful percentage of the indigenous rainforest on one of the nation's larger islands. The results of the failure to do this elsewhere are all too apparent – overlogged hills and wrecked watersheds have led to serious flooding and soil erosion, with crop yields in some areas having fallen below those of several decades ago. The prevalence in the Philippines until relatively recently of a "plunder economy" led to a Klondike-style scramble to strip the country of its resources, especially its minerals, with disastrous environmental results. What happens on Palawan, which in addition to its forest has deposits of chrome, copper and manganese, as well as oil and gas reserves, will be the acid test of whether a corner really has been turned.

Certainly, the increasing number of young Filipinos concerned about the environmental condition of their country gives hope for the future, as does the growing bank of scientific data on the country's surviving forests and their wildlife. Fieldwork and research are raising awareness, both in terms of what is out there and what needs to be done to protect it. Particularly encouraging have been the rediscovery on some islands (Cebu, for example) of bird species previously thought extinct, and the involvement of the international community in conservation work to safeguard endangered habitats and species. At the same time, a change in Filipino political culture has brought greater openness and freedom of expression, which is allowing environmental campaigners to make their voices heard and to challenge the authorities and "big business" when important habitats and wildlife come under threat.

ABOVE **Gone are the days when large flocks of Red-vented Corellas were a common sight across much of the Philippines. Only scattered small groups survive, mostly in the rainforests of Palawan, Bohol and Mindanao.**

RIGHT **Although logging is ostensibly controlled in the Philippines, with a moratorium in place across much of the country, the illegal extraction of timber is a major problem. As elsewhere in the world, much of this activity is fuelled by poverty, with local people often having few economic alternatives.**

OPPOSITE **The indigenous people of Palawan continue traditional cottage industries such as basket weaving. Their presence makes the island a potentially excellent location for the sensitive development of ecotourism, focusing on the rainforest ecosystem, its wildlife and the related human dimension.**

4. The Hidden Mammals of the Vietnamese Rainforests

The rainforests of Vietnam first came to outside attention in a major way in the late 1980s and early '90s with a series of discoveries that were to rock the natural history world. The first chapter in what proved to be a remarkable story – and one that is still ongoing – opened in 1988, when a local hunter was arrested after trying to sell the skin and horn of a female rhino he had shot in the Cat Tien area of southern Vietnam. This proved to be the first confirmed evidence of the continued existence on mainland South-east Asia of the Javan Rhinoceros *Rhinoceros sondaicus*, long considered extinct there and on the brink of global extinction. The world's only known population at that time was in the Ujong Kulon National Park in Java.

Surveys and fieldwork revealed that up to 15 rhinos had somehow hung on in Cat Tien, and the area was gazetted as a rhino sanctuary. The survival of these animals was all the more astonishing given the recent history of the local forests. Much of the area had been logged, with many of the larger trees removed. During the Vietnam War of 1965–75 it was the scene of armed conflict and an attempt by the American air force to flush out Viet Cong fighters by spraying large areas with the defoliant pesticide Agent Orange. In more recent years the human population had grown considerably, with many people taking up residence inside the forest boundaries and actively clearing the vegetation so that they could grow crops. By any standards this appeared to be an unpromising environment for most types of wildlife, let alone a large beast already acknowledged as one of the rarest mammals in the world.

More extraordinary news was to come in 1992, with the announcement of another discovery, this time from Vu Quang, a remote tract of montane rainforest in the north of Vietnam, close to the border with Laos. A visiting team of World Wide Fund for Nature (WWF) researchers noticed

OPPOSITE The Annamite Mountains are home to some of the last pristine tracts of rainforest in Indochina. Whereas at lower altitudes much of the forest has been cleared and converted to farmland, higher and more inaccessible terrain still supports extensive tracts of old-growth forest. Much of this remains little-known scientifically, and biologists are constantly making new discoveries here.

RIGHT The discovery in the late 1980s of a small remnant population of Javan Rhinoceros in Vietnam was truly remarkable. Against all odds the species had somehow survived here, yet sadly since then its numbers have declined to a perilously low ebb.

on display at the houses of local hunters some unusual skulls, bearing long horns and not of an immediately recognizable species. They were then shown skins, whereupon it became clear that here was an animal totally new to science. The body parts were used to make the first description of the Saola or Vu Quang Ox *Pseudoryx nghetinhensis*, an unusual antelope-like bovid deemed so different from any other known species that a new genus was created specially for it. Although familiar to local people, who hunted and trapped it for meat, it was the first large mammal to be "discovered" for over half a century, since the Kouprey *Bos sauveli* (now probably extinct) was found in 1937 in neighbouring Cambodia. Not until 1994 was a live Saola caught and examined, and much remains to be learned about its ecology and behaviour. Estimates of the total population are also guesswork at this stage – numbers may be as low as 250, shared mostly between Vu Quang National Park and the Nakai–Nam Theun National Protected Area over the border in Laos.

Since the Saola's discovery, more new species have been described, and "lost" ones refound, in Cat Tien, Vu Quang and elsewhere in Vietnam. New species of deer, a new rabbit, new reptiles, amphibians, butterflies – the list continues to grow. It is clear that many of the country's surviving rainforests continue to harbour a huge diversity of wildlife and that in some places scientists have only really scratched the surface. The high levels of biodiversity in what is known as the Greater Annamites Ecoregion are explained by its location at the junction of the temperate north and tropical south, a meeting point – or perhaps more accurately an ecological overlap – of flora and fauna converging from different directions. It is also a place where some species have evolved in relative isolation, especially in the more mountainous areas, a factor which helps account for the growing number of endemic species that are now being discovered. The years of war made access to the rainforests particularly difficult – unexploded ordnance and landmines remain a problem today,

OPPOSITE Unknown to science until very recently, this species of tree viper is an example of the remarkable reptile diversity that exists in Vietnam's surviving rainforests. With similar creatures still as yet undescribed by biologists, the case for protecting these forests from further destruction is all the more pressing.

RIGHT Both male and female Saola have the distinctive white facial markings, including the white "eyebrow". The strong neck and hunched shoulders are typical of animals that move constantly through thick undergrowth. This is a young individual with relatively small horns.

for example, including in parts of what is now Cat Tien National Park – and only in recent years has it become possible for scientists to reach some of the more remote locations.

The forests of Vietnam are proving particularly rich in primates, although the numbers of most species are declining and some are in real danger of extinction. Particularly outstanding are the douc langurs, surely among the most attractive of all monkeys. All three species are endangered, including the Grey-shanked Douc *Pygathrix cinerea*, found only in the rainforests of central Vietnam and first brought to the attention of scientists following the confiscation by officials of several males caught there by trappers in 1995–96. Subsequent fieldwork has revealed a surviving population of several hundred Grey-shanked Doucs, although they are threatened by illegal hunting and habitat loss.

The destruction of the native forests is the single biggest conservation problem in Vietnam today. Between 20 and 25 per cent of the country remains forested today, of which roughly half could be regarded as being in pristine, or near-pristine, condition. Reconstruction after many years of war and unrest saw the national demand for timber soar, and more recently the rapid rate of the country's development has placed further demands on already strained natural resources. Economic growth is also generating a vast number of infrastructural projects, such as hydroelectric schemes, with potentially damaging environmental effects. Meanwhile, a rapidly expanding human population, thirsty for agricultural land, is continuing to deplete what little forest remains. The coastal lowlands are now almost devoid of continuous tree cover, and farmers are moving higher into the hills to occupy and clear new plots there.

Many of these issues can be seen on the ground in Cat Tien National Park, and have a direct bearing on the fate of Vietnam's few surviving Javan Rhinos, as well as on the other wildlife found in the park. This includes – it is thought – a handful of Tigers *Panthera tigris*, as well as one of the few remaining Vietnamese herds of Asian Elephant *Elephas maximus*, probably numbering no more than 20 animals (only about 100 individuals survive in the entire country). Whether the

BELOW **Vietnam's rainforests are home to some of the world's most handsome and endangered primates, such as the endemic Red-shanked Douc *Pygathrix nemaeus*. Its numbers have fallen dramatically as a result of habitat destruction and poaching for the illegal pet trade.**

OPPOSITE **Noted for its extraordinary long and bushy tail, Delacour's Langur *Trachypithecus delacouri* is under severe threat of extinction. Its bones, organs and tissues are valued in traditional Chinese medicine and hunting has reduced the population by 50 per cent since the early 1990s. Fewer than 300 survive today.**

populations of these species – and, indeed, of the Javan Rhino – are viable at such low levels is doubtful. The park covers 74,000 hectares (183,000 acres), roughly 50 per cent of which comprises evergreen (mostly dipterocarp) or semi-evergreen (mainly *Lagerstroemia* spp.) forest, with a further 40 per cent covered by bamboo thickets. The park contains a substantial part of the Dong Nai river basin and the remaining 10 per cent of its area is wetland and grassland. Sections of the forest are regenerating following logging activity and the impact of Agent Orange, although certain areas that were badly affected by the pesticide have yet to recover, some 40 years after the event.

The park's rhinos are confined to the dense tracts of bamboo and rattan covering the steep slopes of the Cat Loc sector. This is not typical habitat for this species, and they were probably forced to retreat up here from their preferred environment – low-lying rainforest with open glades for grazing – in the face of increasing human pressure. The Javan Rhino stands on the very brink of extinction, with fewer than 60 thought to survive on Java and no more than eight in Vietnam, according to the latest figures – a decrease from the number estimated at the time of their rediscovery here. The Vietnamese animals are recognized as a separate subspecies, *Rhinoceros sondaicus annamiticus*, and are 30–40 per cent smaller than the Javanese population, from which scientists believe they are sufficiently distinct to make cross-breeding impossible. Adults stand 130–150 centimetres (50–60 inches) at the shoulder and can weigh up to 1,500 kilograms (3,300 pounds), but the animals are very rarely seen. Much of what is known about them and their habits comes from study of their tracks and dung, although camera traps have been used to photograph animals as they visit the salt-licks and wallows that are an essential part of their lives.

BELOW LEFT AND RIGHT The Annamite highlands continue to yield species of plant that are totally new to science. In 2007 the discoveries in Vietnam's central 'Green Corridor' included (left) *Anoectochilus annamensis*, a shade-loving orchid with exquisitely patterned leaves, and (right) the highly unusual *Aspidistra nicolai*.

54 ASIA

The rhinos face a range of threats, from competition for grazing with the park's population of Gaur *Bos gaurus* to the impact of certain types of invasive vegetation, which restrict the growth of species on which the rhino depends. However, the single greatest factor jeopardizing the rhino population is undoubtedly the human presence. Some 10,000 people live within the park boundaries, including some in the sector inhabited by the rhinos, with a further 200,000 in the buffer zone adjacent to the park. Many are farmers seeking to establish plantations of lucrative cash crops such as cashews; the relocation of these people from the park's "core zone" to appropriate land outside is a conservation priority for locally active organizations such as WWF, alongside the recruitment and training of forest rangers and the implementation of community education programmes.

Although there has been much progress in recent years, improved conservation awareness is vital if Vietnam is to save what remains of its forests and their superb flora and fauna. A visit to a local market is not for the faint-hearted visitor from overseas, with many animals – both alive and dead – on sale, whether as pets, for trophy hunters or simply for the cooking pot. As economic prosperity brings improved living standards, so the killing of wild animals for food should decline, but the commercial trade in wildlife – including endangered species – is a huge problem across South-east Asia. Vietnam continues to function as a supplier, consumer and broker in this process, but since much of the traffic is domestic in nature it falls outside the provisions of the Convention on International Trade in Endangered Species of Wild Fauna and Flora (CITES). Unless concerted action is taken soon, this trade risks emptying the country's forests of many of the species that in recent years have made this one of the most exciting wildlife stories of the last half-century.

ABOVE **Edwards's Pheasant** *Lophura edwardsi* **is endemic to the rainforests of central Vietnam but is an elusive and little-known species. Numbers in the wild are perilously low, but a captive breeding programme – of which this female forms part – holds out hope for the future.**

5. The Tigers and Elephants of Sumatra's Shrinking Rainforests

The world's sixth-largest island, Sumatra was still largely covered in rainforest at the turn of the twentieth century. Lightly populated at that time, the island's estimated 160,000 square kilometres (62,000 square miles) of rainforest supported large populations of a variety of forest-dwelling mammals, including the endemic Sumatran Tiger *Panthera tigris sumatrae* and Sumatran Orang-utan *Pongo abelii*, as well as the local race of Asian Elephant *Elephas maximus sumatranus*. Since then, a rate of deforestation probably faster than anywhere else in the world has reduced Sumatra's forest coverage to a mere 5,000 square kilometres (1,950 square miles), an alarming trend but one that is sadly repeated across much of Indonesia. Over one-third of the country's forests were destroyed between 1985 and 1997, a period during which they were increasingly carved up into logging concessions and awarded to the allies and supporters of the country's then head of state, President Suharto.

The pattern of logging and destruction on Sumatra is a familiar one and mirrors the pattern found elsewhere in South-east Asia and, indeed, beyond. Armed with official concessions, loggers will first forge access roads into a forest and proceed to extract the most valuable hardwoods for sale as timber. Illegal loggers then move in, concentrating on clear-felling those trees that remain and, in this case, sending most of them off to be pulped for paper manufacture. In recent years the destruction of Sumatra's forests has been largely fuelled by the high demand for paper, mainly from Europe, Japan and the United States. The two largest pulp mills in the world are located

BELOW **Habitat loss and increasing conflict with humans mean that the future for Sumatran Tigers in the wild is uncertain.**

RIGHT **With their forest habitat increasingly denuded and fragmented, wild elephants in Sumatra are increasingly turning to agricultural land to find food.**

on the island, kept busy by a constant supply of timber drawn from Sumatra's dwindling forests. Once the land is stripped of almost all its trees, it will usually be put to agricultural use, either by opportunistic farmers and squatters scraping a living from what are often poor soils with low crop yields, or by commercial concerns dealing in more lucrative commodities such as palm oil. In both cases the forest remnants – often simply scrub by this point – are often fired in an attempt to totally clear the site and allow the planting of new crops.

The horror stories coming out of Indonesia in the late 1990s – including the shocking images of smoke billowing up from what was left of Sumatra's wrecked forests and blanketing Singapore and much of Malaysia with smog for months – prompted concerted action from several directions, including the Indonesian government. One positive outcome was the establishment in 2004 of Tesso Nilo National Park, one of the largest surviving fragments of lowland rainforest on Sumatra. The forest at Tesso Nilo was being clear-felled at such a rate that it would have been entirely destroyed within a decade, but the logging licence was returned to the Indonesian government and an initial 38,756 hectares (95,766 acres) subsequently declared a protected area. In 2006 the park was extended to 100,000 hectares (247,000 acres). It represents one of the most important botanic sites in Sumatra, with over 4,000 plant species recorded, as well as supporting significant populations of tiger and elephant, both of which are at serious risk of extinction on the island unless effective conservation measures are taken soon.

The Sumatran form is the world's smallest surviving tiger, following the extinction during the twentieth century of the separate races that had evolved on Bali and Java. An adult male will weigh up to 140 kilograms (310 pounds) and reach 60 centimetres (24 inches) at the shoulder – compared to approximately 200 kilograms (440 pounds) and 115 centimetres (45 inches) respectively in the case of the largest race, the Siberian or Amur Tiger *Panthera tigris altaica*. The demise of Sumatra's forests has been matched by a steep decline in its tiger population, now regarded as critically endangered, with only 350 or so animals estimated to be surviving in the wild. The pressures on them are intense, and while habitat loss is probably the most critical factor affecting the species, poaching also remains a major threat. According to the World Wide Fund

ABOVE **Sumatra has seen some of the most dramatic deforestation of anywhere in the world, with rainforest clearance at its peak during the 1980s and '90s. Although the rate of destruction has slowed since then, much of the island shows the visible scars of carpet logging.**

for Nature, some 116 tigers were killed in central and southern Sumatra between 1998 and 2002. Some of these deaths were due to tiger–human conflict, with tigers increasingly forced into close, and often fatal, proximity to Sumatra's rapidly expanding population. With undisturbed tracts of forest increasingly rare, and their prey base falling, tigers are forced to live in marginal habitat such as in secondary forest and even on agricultural land, where conflict with humans becomes inevitable. In such circumstances it is hard to see how the island's tigers can survive unless more tracts of forest such as Tesso Nilo, an important stronghold for the species, are protected effectively.

Tesso Nilo is also home to another mammal that is the smallest race of its species – the Sumatran form of Asian Elephant, of which fewer than 2,000 animals survive in the wild. These are scattered across the island in increasingly dwindling populations, vulnerable to the continuing destruction and fragmentation of their forest home and drawn into potentially dangerous confrontations with humans. Deprived of access to their traditional feeding areas – often now destroyed or surrounded by farmland or commercial plantations – the beleaguered elephants are increasingly forced into populated areas and onto farmland, where they damage crops and come into conflict with local villagers. Ripe crops are an irresistible temptation for elephants, and crop-raiding had become a particular problem at Tesso Nilo, where wild elephants would leave the forest at night and cause extensive damage on adjacent farmland.

RIGHT TOP AND BOTTOM **Sumatra's tigers are particularly elusive and rarely seen. Photographing them is virtually impossible without the use of camera traps, which along with the recording of tracks and other physical signs offer the best hope of counting individuals and assessing population levels.**

An interesting solution was devised to deal with the situation. Since 2006 a "flying squad" of a motor bike, jeep and four captive elephants has been used to drive parties of wild elephants back into the forest. Pipe cannons and bright lights – to which the tame elephants are habituated – are used to cajole the crop-raiders out of the fields and back into the forest. If this does not work, the captive elephants and their mahouts move in among the wild animals, physically pushing them back if necessary. While this may be an effective method of wild elephant control, the core problem is not going to go away: how can large and highly mobile mammals such as elephants co-exist in future with an increasing human population that is demanding more and more of the elephants' natural habitat?

Elsewhere in Sumatra, international efforts are helping to save the island's remaining rainforests. In 2007 the UK's Royal Society for the Protection of Birds (RSPB) joined forces with Birdlife International and the local conservation body Burung Indonesia to outbid logging companies and secure a 100-year management concession over an important tract of lowland rainforest at Harapan in central Sumatra. The forest is known to support at least 267 species of bird (although the true total may be in excess of 300), many of which are highly localized and declining, as well as important populations of tiger and elephant and other vulnerable mammals such as Sun Bear *Helarctos malayanus* and Clouded Leopard *Neofelis nebulosa*. The length of the concession should enable the forest to recover fully from the logging that had already taken place there in previous decades, and the forest's protected status should help ensure that it can continue to provide a home for its traditional human inhabitants, the Batin Sembilan tribe, who have historically depended on forest products such as rattan, honey and rubber, and will now also be offered the opportunity to work as forest guides and wildlife wardens.

BELOW AND OPPOSITE **The rainforest at Harapan supports a wide range of birdlife. This includes the scarce and localized Lesser Adjutant** *Leptoptilos javanicus* **(below) alongside classic rainforest species such as Red-naped Trogon** *Harpactes kasumba* **(opposite).**

While such projects certainly hold out hope for the future, the current situation for Sumatra's rainforests and the wildlife they support is worrying. In 2007 horrendous pictures emerged – via a camera trap set up in Tesso Nilo park – of an adult tiger that had lost the lower part of one of its front legs, almost certainly as a result of getting caught in a snare, from which it had extricated itself by somehow scratching or chewing off its paw. Although the animal appeared to be in satisfactory health, its ability to continue to hunt effectively and feed itself must be in question. This incident serves to underline the risks faced by wild animals in Sumatra, where poaching, illegal logging and agricultural encroachment are all widespread, even within protected areas such as Tesso Nilo. Meanwhile, population pressure on the island continues to intensify, with many people having relocated to Sumatra in recent decades from more highly populated islands such as Java. The prevailing combination of generally weak law enforcement, corrupt officials and widespread poverty is an unpromising cocktail for successful wildlife conservation.

BELOW **Harapan Forest** showing the large number of emergents protruding above the main canopy layer. Primary forest such as this is increasingly rare on Sumatra.

RIGHT **The Clouded Leopard** is thinly distributed across Sumatra in surviving stands of old-growth rainforest. Numbers have declined as a result of habitat loss and illegal hunting and trapping.

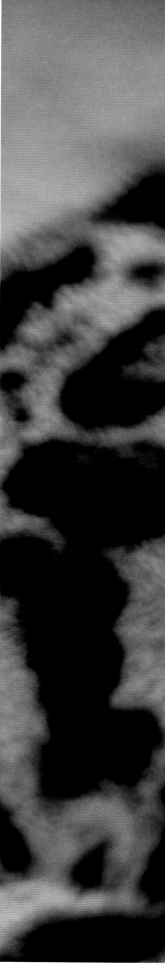

6. The Sundarban Mangroves of Bangladesh and India

The Sundarbans are one of the last great wildernesses on the Indian subcontinent. Covering some 10,000 square kilometres (3,850 square miles), these vast tracts of mangrove forest and associated habitats are part of the largest fluvio-alluvial delta in the world, formed by the deposition of countless tons of sediment carried down from the Himalayas by the rivers Ganges, Brahmaputra and Meghna and their tributaries.

Subject also to the constant processes of tidal erosion and accretion, the delta comprises many alluvial islands and sandbanks, contained within a complex network of interconnecting channels. Some of these channels are several kilometres wide. Water levels are largely dictated by the movements of the tide, and most of the channels are therefore saline, especially in areas where they have become cut off from freshwater sources by the accumulation of silt and by dams and barrages built on the edges of the delta. The physical processes of the tides – the average rise and fall of which ranges from 2 metres (6.5 feet) to over 5 metres (16.5 feet) in places – are the key dynamic in the Sundarbans ecosystem, and an ever-present factor in the lives of the wildlife and people that live here.

Sixty per cent of the Sundarbans lies within Bangladesh, and the remaining 40 per cent is across the international border in the Indian state of West Bengal. Core areas on both sides are listed as World Heritage Sites. There are various types of mangrove vegetation in the delta, with a distinct sequence of successional habitats resulting from the constantly changing conditions and levels of salinity, as different plant communities take advantage of the environments best-suited to their requirements.

RIGHT **Invertebrates are among the least-studied aspects of the flora and fauna of the Sundarbans. Some groups show high rates of endemism, and species new to science doubtless await discovery here. Butterflies are well represented and include species such as the Crimson Rose** *Atrophaneura hector*, **a type of swallowtail.**

OPPOSITE **The Sundarbans are dissected by many kilometres of tidal channels, the levels of which are subject to considerable fluctuation. Human access to much of the area is therefore by boat, and the local wildlife is equally forced to take on a semi-aquatic existence.**

Between approximately one-third and one-half of the total area is under water at any one time, with the erosion and accretion processes caused by the tide ensuring that this is an environment that is in a constant state of flux. Newly formed land is rapidly colonized by pioneer and highly salt-tolerant species such as *Avicennia* spp. and Keora *Sonneratia apetala*. Kankra *Bruguiera gymnorrhiza* is common in areas that are subject to regular flooding.

On areas of more-established and drier land, the climax vegetation includes Gengwa or Gewa *Excoecaria agallocha*, Goran *Ceriops decandra* and notably *Heritiera fomes*, known as Sundari or Sundri, and from which the name "Sundarbans" is most likely derived (*ban* being the Bengali word for forest). Sundari trees can grow as tall as 25 metres (80 feet), but the largest specimens have mostly been felled. The wood is highly prized for a range of uses, from bridge construction and boat-building through to telegraph poles and flooring. Meanwhile, palm species such as Golpata or Nypa Palm *Nypa fruticans* and Hental Palm *Phoenix paludosa* are common along the waterways.

Approximately 330 species of plant, 42 mammals, 35 reptiles, 125 fish and 300 birds have been recorded from the Sundarbans, which have long been renowned as an area rich in wildlife. Hunting accounts from a century or more ago describe an impressive array of quarry animals, including species such as Javan Rhinoceros *Rhinoceros sondaicus*, Wild Water Buffalo *Bubalus bubalis*, Hog Deer *Axis procinus* and Swamp Deer *Cervus duvauceli*. All of these are now extinct in the region as a result of overhunting and habitat changes, but the area's top predator, the Tiger *Panthera tigris*, has survived here in good numbers.

With tiger numbers in freefall virtually everywhere else, and with the latest figures for India (based on a 2006 survey) giving an estimated total figure of only 1,411 tigers for the whole of the country – down from 3,642 only five years earlier – the Sundarbans tiger population is particularly important. No accurate figures exist, but there are probably between 300 and 500 tigers living here. Given the unique local terrain, *khal* (creek) surveys are used to assess relative tiger abundance based on tracks in the mud. Tigers have also been radio-collared in an attempt to establish average home range size and thereby the carrying capacity of the wider area.

The Sundarbans are the only part of the world where tigers live in a mangrove forest and where they have evolved a semi-amphibious way of life, regularly commuting across the channels between islands and on occasions even having been reported swimming in the open sea. The area also has the dubious distinction of being the location of more tiger attacks on humans than anywhere else in the world. The tigers here have a reputation for being particularly aggressive, with various non-scientific explanations (such as the aggravating effect of a saline environment on the tigers' temper) traditionally offered to explain the high incidence of attacks. Recent research reveals, however, that these attacks are due more to factors such as increasing levels of human intrusion and habitat degradation than to any more fanciful notions.

Whatever the reasons, human–tiger conflict in the Sundarbans has two main sources. Most human casualties (up to 100 annually result from villagers venturing onto forested

RIGHT TOP AND BOTTOM **Mangroves** are the iconic plant species of the Sundarbans, which contains the world's largest mangrove forest. Their complex root networks help secure soil that would otherwise be washed away and thereby promote the establishment of other vegetation and, ultimately, the creation of permanently dry land. These root webs also serve as a host environment for a range of marine organisms and are especially important as nurseries for fish. Mangroves are among the world's most rapidly disappearing habitats, with up to one-third having been destroyed in the past three decades.

OPPOSITE **The tigers of the** Sundarbans are totally at home in water, regularly swimming between islands and across channels. Highly elusive animals, the tracks they leave in the waterside mud are one of the few ways in which their numbers can be estimated.

islands to gather wood and honey, but tigers also stray out of the forest into nearby villages and attack livestock. In these situations the tigers themselves risk being injured and killed. Various measures have been trialled to minimize conflict, including the installation of nets to prevent tigers from entering villages, the use of face masks for villagers to wear on their backs when out in the forest (tigers appear less likely to attack a human face) and the placement of automated models of humans, to deter tigers from entering certain areas. However, educational work, aimed at training local people on how to avoid dangerous situations with tigers, is paramount, as is helping villagers to find alternative sources of income and economic livelihood that do not depend on their entering the forest. This is increasingly important as the human population expands and places unsustainable pressure on the forest's natural resources.

Conflicts do still arise, however. In February 2008, for example, a female tiger was hounded by an angry mob of people after wandering into a village and was rescued by forest guards only after it had been chased up a tree, which the villagers had then set on fire. The traumatized and by now highly dangerous animal was finally tranquilized, rescued and treated for its injuries before being relocated. This incident serves to underline how fragile is the relationship between the human inhabitants of the Sundarbans and one of the world's most endangered big cats.

Attacks on humans aside, the largest prey available to tigers in the Sundarbans is the Spotted Deer or Chital *Axis axis*, which is very common here. The tigers also regularly take Wild Boar *Sus scrofa* and Rhesus Macaques *Macaca mulatta*, and have even been seen feeding on fish. In other parts of their range tigers will normally take much larger prey than that available in the Sundarbans – an adult animal requires an average of 5 kilograms (11 pounds) of meat per day – and the restricted choices here may help explain the relatively small size of Sundarban tigers. They may be only slightly larger on average than the smallest surviving subspecies, the Sumatran Tiger.

Other wildlife in the Sundarbans includes Fishing Cat *Felis viverrinus* as well as both Smooth-coated Otter *Lutrogale perspicillata* and Oriental Small-clawed Otter *Aonyx cinerea* and some impressive specimens of Estuarine Crocodile *Crocodylus porosus*. Birdlife is abundant and in addition to resident species (nine species of kingfisher and the rare Masked Finfoot

OPPOSITE **A magnificent Spotted Deer stag. Many thousands of these deer live in the forests of the Sundarbans, providing abundant prey for the tiger population. Their distinctive alarm call, a high-pitched yelp, is often a sign that a tiger or other predator is in the area.**

ABOVE **Techniques to reduce human-tiger conflict are constantly being reappraised. Effigies wrapped in electric wire are now eschewed in favour of alternatives such as community-based education and training aimed at minimizing exposure to risk.**

RIGHT **A rare view of a Sundarbans tiger. Exactly how many live here is uncertain, but this is undoubtedly home to one of the world's last concentrations of this magnificent creature. They have been helped by the difficult terrain, which has traditionally discouraged poachers.**

Heliopais personata, for example) includes important numbers of migratory duck and waders, which stop off and refuel in the delta en route to and from their breeding grounds in northern Asia.

For centuries, if not thousands of years, the mangrove forests of the Sundarbans have acted as both a stabilizing force and a safety barrier for the settlements and agricultural land that lie inland from the delta, protecting these areas from cyclones and flooding, in addition to providing valuable resources such as timber, fuelwood, thatching material, honey and fish.

Today, however, there are many signs that this unique ecosystem is in trouble. Although there are no permanent human residents within the core protected areas of the Sundarbans, population pressure from the many millions of people living in the wider delta is resulting in the degradation of much of the habitat. Overfishing is a major problem, with catches now declining rapidly, and has been exacerbated by the recent proliferation of commercial shrimp farms. The shrimp larvae are largely collected from the wild through the use of fine-meshed nets, which result in high losses of fish fry. A further issue is the destruction of mangrove forest to make space for more paddyfields. As the forest shrinks, so the pressure on what remains intensifies, with the more accessible areas of forest now seriously depleted of their wood stock and struggling to regenerate.

A further issue is the generally weak enforcement of existing protective regulations on both sides of the India–Bangladesh border. Although this problem is partly explained by the difficulty of the terrain, it is exacerbated by a traditional lack of coordination between the two sides. Whilst improved collaboration is now taking place on a research level, there is still no single overview of what is, of course, a single ecosystem.

However, the single biggest long-term threat to the world's largest mangrove forest is the rising sea levels caused by climate change. Saltwater encroachment has a drastic effect on vegetation, thereby confining the wildlife to increasingly restricted patches of habitat in which there may be inadequate resources for survival. By 2020 it is estimated that 15 per cent of the Sundarbans' most vulnerable areas will be lost to the sea. Meanwhile, the potential impact of the cyclones that regularly batter this stretch of the Bengal coastline will become greater as the various habitat components deteriorate and the protective effect of the mangrove forests diminishes. The full implications of the November 2007 cyclone, for example, which caused damage to 30 per cent or so of the Sundarbans, are still not fully clear.

BELOW Waterbirds abound in the Sundarbans and include nine species of kingfisher. The Brown-winged Kingfisher *Perlargopsis amauroptera* is a mangrove specialist and still common here, although elsewhere in South-east Asia it has suffered local declines as a result of habitat loss.

OPPOSITE With much of the area seasonally underwater, the wildlife of the Sundarbans must constantly adapt to changing water levels. During the monsoon animals are more concentrated on the drier islands, but they soon move out once the waters recede to reveal fresh grazing areas.

OPPOSITE The local human inhabitants have traditionally utilized many of the forest products for their everyday needs. Materials such as palm are still harvested and used in house construction, for example. However, as population pressure builds, the issue of sustainability becomes paramount.

THE SUNDARBAN MANGROVES OF BANGLADESH AND INDIA **71**

7. The Limestone Forests of Khao Sok, Thailand

In the mid-twentieth century an estimated 80 per cent of Thailand was covered in indigenous forest. That figure has now declined to less than 20 per cent and, although logging was officially banned across the country in the late 1980s, illegal timber extraction and clearance for agriculture continue to threaten what remains. Much of the surviving forest is highly fragmented and populations of the iconic animals for which the country was once famous – notably Asian Elephant *Elephas maximus* and Tiger *Panthera tigris* – are seriously depleted. However, the country has the most extensive network of national parks and protected areas in South-east Asia, covering 60 per cent or so of the surviving natural habitats.

One of the most important wildlife areas in southern Thailand is Khao Sok National Park, located on the Thai/Malay Peninsula, 150 kilometres (95 miles) north of Phuket. Covering 739 square kilometres (285 square miles), the park extends over a section of the mountain ridge that separates the peninsula's west and east coasts. Together with two adjacent wildlife sanctuaries and two other neighbouring national parks, it protects the second-largest contiguous tract of forest – after Malaysia's Taman Negara National Park – remaining between Bangkok and Singapore, covering some 4,000 square kilometres (1,550 square miles) in total.

Scenically, this is an outstanding landscape. Dense evergreen forest carpets a range of mudstone hills studded by dramatic limestone or "karst" outcrops, reaching as high as 960 metres (3,150 feet) and with exposed pillars and pinnacles of white rock rising out of the canopy. These configurations, which can look almost architectural in character, are as impressive as the more famous stacks in Phang Nga Bay to the south, and are the remnants of a prehistoric coral reef system that once stretched across much of this region when it lay beneath the sea. There are also extensive networks of caves which, together with the largely inaccessible nature of much of the terrain, led to the area becoming a refuge for Communist insurgents during the 1960s and '70s. Paradoxically, this helped protect the area's wildlife, as most people were unsurprisingly reluctant to enter the forest to hunt or to convert land to agriculture.

RIGHT The dramatic limestone scenery of Khao Sok makes this park a popular destination with mainstream tourists. Wildlife enthusiasts come to enjoy its prolific birdlife and the chance to see some of Thailand's increasingly scarce forest animals.

OPPOSITE The White-handed Gibbon remains relatively common in Khao Sok. Individual coloration can vary from blond, as here, to deep chocolate brown (see page 75), but all have the white ring around the face, as well as the distinctive white hands and feet.

ABOVE Heavy rainfall and high levels of humidity are characteristic of the rainforest environment, especially in the early morning. The powerful sun can soon break through, but the process of convection often triggers heavy showers by the late afternoon.

Following an improvement in security, Khao Sok was declared a national park in 1980. However, its northern section was severely disrupted two years later by the construction of Rachabrapah Dam across the Pasaeng River and the creation of the 165-square-kilometre (65-square-mile) Chiew Larn Reservoir. The skeletal forms of what were once huge forest trees still rise from the waters as a reminder of what disappeared beneath the flood a quarter of a century ago. Much of the area's wildlife was drowned, despite a limited rescue operation, and it is certain that some species have never recovered from the disturbance and loss of habitat. However, the reservoir is now incorporated within the park, and boat trips on it can provide some of the best opportunities for watching birds, particularly in the forest edge that runs along its shores.

There are many interesting vegetation types in the park, not least those associated with the limestone areas. Although wet evergreen forest covers most of the lower sections of the park, with many fine dipterocarps and a classic understorey of ferns and palms, on the limestone escarpments and outcrops these are replaced by more drought-resistant species. The more diminutive trees and shrubs reflect the less forgiving environment here, and are clamped on to the sun-bleached and desiccated rock, their roots straining into the cracks and crevices to try to reach moisture. These "sky island" habitats are home to a range of highly localized plants and invertebrates, some of them endemic. Meanwhile, down below, the very different conditions associated with the park's plentiful gorges and waterfalls also provide a plethora of habitat niches for reptiles and amphibians in particular.

It is in the proximity of water that one has the best chance of seeing Khao Sok's largest – and the world's longest – snake, the Reticulated Python *Python reticulatus*. Adult specimens regularly reach lengths of 7 metres (20 feet) and giants in excess of 10 metres (30 feet) have been claimed. While in terms of bulk this species is not as massive as the thicker-bodied anacondas from South America, it is a formidable predator nonetheless. Prey varies from rodents, reptiles and birds up to animals as large as Sun Bear *Helarctos malayanus* and Leopard *Panthera pardus*, although more

OPPOSITE TOP The beautiful markings of the Reticulated Python serve as excellent camouflage on the forest floor, but have also resulted in this species being hunted intensively across much of its range. Despite being ostensibly protected, many thousands are killed each year for their skin and body parts.

OPPOSITE BOTTOM Gibbons can be hard to see as they swing by their arms through the canopy, but sometimes it is possible to catch a glimpse as they run, arms held partly aloft, along horizontal branches. When at full swing, they can move at speeds of up to 55 kilometres (34 miles) per hour and cover as much as 15 metres (49 feet) in a single movement.

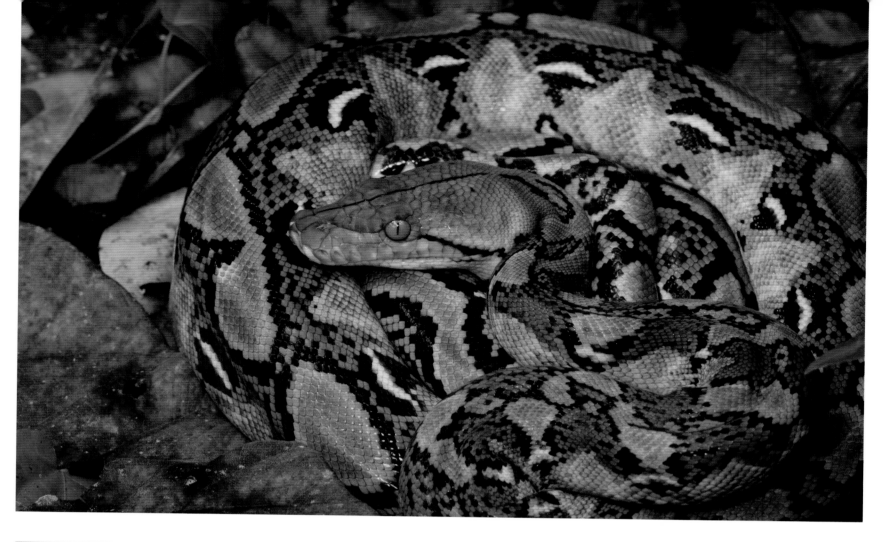

normal prey in Khao Sok would be deer, wild pig and smaller carnivores such as civets. Pythons are excellent swimmers and readily take to water; younger snakes are predominantly arboreal, hunting birds and tree-climbing mammals but slowly becoming more terrestrial as they grow in size and require larger prey. When not hunting, adult snakes usually lie up in a cave or hollowed-out tree root, often near water.

Forty-eight mammal species have been recorded from the park, but the status of many – especially Tiger and Asian Elephant – is unclear. Very small numbers of both species may still survive in the more remote areas of forest, but their populations may well have fallen below the point of viability. Both Banteng *Bos javanicus* and Gaur *Bos gaurus* are present, as are Malayan Tapir *Tapirus indicus*, but all are elusive and rarely encountered by casual visitors. Large species such as these have declined dramatically across all of their Asian range as a result of habitat loss and hunting, with many instances of local extinction. Even in places where they still survive they have become largely nocturnal, with tracks and dung often the only evidence of their presence. One particularly interesting mammal in Khao Sok is the Serow *Capricornis sumatrensis*, a secretive goat-like animal found mainly on the limestone outcrops.

Meanwhile, the most readily seen mammals in the park are probably bats, of which at least 38 species have been recorded here. In the evening many thousands – quite possibly millions – stream out of the park's caves to hunt over the reservoir and surrounding forest. Night-time also offers the best opportunity for finding one of the world's most enigmatic primates, the Slow Loris. Two species may occur in Khao Sok: the Asian Slow Loris *Nycticebus bengalensis*, and the slightly smaller Sunda Slow Loris *Nycticebus coucang*. Both are very similar in habits and appearance, and may well hybridize. Unlike most other primates, slow lorises are strictly nocturnal, moving slowly and deliberately through the tree canopy and undergrowth in search of fruits, flower nectar, gum and sap, as well as invertebrates, young birds, small reptiles and amphibians. Interestingly, they are also one of the world's very few poisonous mammals – glands on their elbows exude a poison, which the loris licks up, coating its teeth. It can then deliver a painful bite, with the resulting wound swelling and itching or aching. Mother slow lorises will lick their young with the poison, presumably to ward off predators.

During daylight hours Dusky Langurs *Trachypithecus obscurus* are a relatively common sight in the forest. They are usually found in family groups of between five and 20 individuals, led by one or more adult males and occupying a home range of up to 20 hectares (50 acres). White-handed Gibbons *Hylobates lar* are also frequently seen, and certainly heard, their whooping "song" a regular but always thrilling component of the forest dawn chorus. Birdlife is prolific

FAR LEFT AND LEFT The understorey at Khao Sok contains many palms and ferns, below which lives one of the park's most colourful birds, the Banded Pitta. Like other members of its family, this striking species spends most of its time foraging among the leaf litter on the forest floor. The best hope of seeing any pitta is usually by chancing upon one as it crosses a path or track, usually bounding along on its longish legs with the erect posture characteristic of this family.

here, with almost 200 species recorded from the park. These include several species of hornbill, with Great *Buceros bicornis*, Helmeted *B. vigil* and Bushy-crested Hornbill *Anorrhinus galeritus* usually the most obvious, as well as numerous kingfishers. Khao Sok is also considered by many birders to be one of the best places in Thailand for seeing the stunning Banded Pitta *Pitta guajana*.

One of the most breathtaking – in every sense of the word – natural history treasures of Khao Sok is the remarkable *Rafflesia kerrii*. First collected from the area in the 1920s, this species was mistakenly labelled as one already described from Malaysia. Its true identity remained undiscovered until over half a century later, when a re-examination of the original dried specimen revealed that it was in fact new to science. Fieldwork at Khao Sok led to the rediscovery of the living plant, which appears to be not uncommon in certain locations although its appearance above ground is as fitful as it is dramatic. Members of the Rafflesiaceae are parasitic, spending much of their life cycle as tiny filaments growing inside the roots of vines of the genus *Tetrastigma*. Rafflesias have no leaves, but periodically – and erratically, as "flowering" does not take place every year – buds develop and then erupt through the roots of the host plant to appear above ground among the forest floor leaf litter. These buds then swell to the size of cabbages and open into extraordinary flowers; in the case of *R. kerrii* these can reach 70 centimetres (30 inches) or more in diameter, making it one of the largest flowers in the world. As if their appearance were not impressive enough, the male flowers exude an unpleasant aroma not unlike the smell of putrefying flesh. This serves to attract carrion flies, which are the pollinating agent for this species.

ABOVE **Rafflesias are among the most extraordinary of all plants. The spasmodic appearance of their flowers reflects the complexity of the symbiotic arrangement they maintain with their host. Conditions must be just right, or an individual plant will not bloom.**

AUSTRALASIA

The climatic and geographical diversity of Australasia make it one of the world's most fascinating regions for wildlife. Long periods of ecological isolation have seen the evolution of special groups such as marsupials and helped ensure that rates of endemism are among the highest recorded anywhere. Rainforests are particularly well represented here, from the vast tropical lowland and montane rainforests of New Guinea, still largely unexplored by biologists and where extraordinary new creatures doubtless await scientific discovery, to the Queensland Wet Tropics, where cassowaries and tree kangaroos maintain their only toehold in Australia. To the south lie the temperate rainforests of the islands of Tasmania and New Zealand, where conservation work is underway to help restore the damage wrought on vulnerable indigenous wildlife and vegetation by introduced alien species.

LEFT The Green Tree Python *Morelia viridis* is widely distributed through the rainforests of New Guinea and associated islands. It also occurs in a small strip of forest on Cape York Peninsula in northern Queensland. Individuals only assume the dramatic green coloration on adulthood; juveniles are yellow or orange.

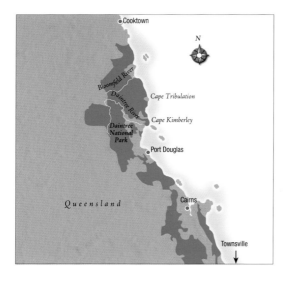

8. The Cassowaries of the Queensland Rainforest, Australia

The so-called "Wet Tropics" of northern Queensland in Australia, extending for some 450 kilometres (280 miles) along the coast between Cooktown and Townsville, were declared a World Heritage Site in 1988. Covering almost 895,000 hectares (2.1 million acres), and including open eucalypt woodland as well as wetlands and mangrove forest, this is foremost an area of outstanding tropical rainforest, and probably one of the oldest of its type in the world. The landscape here was formed during the period of the ancient supercontinent Gondwanaland, dating back to the Precambrian era, some 500 million years ago. At that time lush tropical rainforest covered much of what is today Australia, but subsequent climate changes prompted the contraction of this rainforest and the ensuing extinction of many of the plants and animals that lived there.

However, the particular geological configuration and microclimates made this part of north-east Queensland, with its cloud-enshrouded peaks, isolated moist valleys and high levels of rainfall (as much as 7,000 millimetres/275 inches annually), a refuge for many of the specialist forms of plants and wildlife that had evolved in the Precambrian rainforest environment. Some of these species

LEFT Tree ferns are among the iconic plant groups of the Wet Tropics. Occurring in both tropical and temperate conditions, members of the family Cyatheaceae have remained essentially unchanged for millions of years and serve as a reminder that rainforests are among the oldest of ecosystems.

RIGHT Encountering a cassowary in the rainforest is always an exciting experience. They will often stand motionless, watching what is going on, before suddenly taking fright and dashing off through the vegetation at high speed. Caution should always be shown in their presence, as they can be unpredictable.

survive in the Wet Tropics today in a form little changed from that of millions of years ago – 12 of the world's 19 most primitive plant families are represented here, for example. In total, over 3,000 plant species have been recorded, alongside one-third of Australia's 315 mammal species. Unsurprisingly, rates of endemism are high, and many species of wildlife maintain their only toehold in Australia in these forests. Equally significantly, this is the only place in Australia where an aboriginal rainforest culture existed into relatively recent times. The Kuku Yalanji are the area's traditional inhabitants, historically subsisting as hunter-gatherers in what was a highly productive environment providing all of their needs.

Some of the most interesting and accessible areas of rainforest are in Daintree National Park, where an excellent range of typical plants and wildlife can be seen, although finding some of the more unusual inhabitants requires a combination of luck and persistence. The park is home to some of the Wet Tropics' rarest and most localized species, with remarkable plants such as *Idiospermum australiense*, a relict species of tree that was believed to have been extinct for millions of years until its extraordinary rediscovery in 1972. Birdlife is prolific, with over 250 species recorded. Mammals include two species of tree kangaroo and one of Australia's few truly carnivorous mammals, the endangered Spotted-tailed Quoll *Dasyurus maculatus gracilis*. Several species of ringtail possum

BELOW Exploring the Daintree area is most profitably done on foot, with networks of trails leading through some of the most interesting areas in terms of vegetation and wildlife. Seasonal riverbeds and gullies are always worth checking out for reptiles and amphibians.

ABOVE The Daintree River (or Cinereous) Ringtail Possum was formerly considered to be conspecific with the Herbert River Ringtail, which is a darker colour. The two were formally "split" into separate species within the last 20 years. Both are endemic to the rainforests of Queensland.

OPPOSITE Buttress roots are a key characteristic of many species of rainforest tree. They help anchor and support large trees in what are often poor soils, but also fulfil other functions, such as helping the tree absorb nutrients and minerals from a wider area than would otherwise be possible. The areas between the individual buttresses are also valuable micro-habitats for invertebrates and plants.

also occur here, including the endemic Daintree River Ringtail Possum *Pseudochirulus cinereus*, which was described as a separate species only as recently as 1989 and is almost entirely restricted to the river catchment system.

Its banks largely draped in classic rainforest vegetation, the Daintree River is particularly renowned as the home of another species little changed in appearance or behaviour from prehistoric times – the Estuarine or Saltwater Crocodile *Crocodylus porosus*. "Salties", as they are known locally, have increased here in recent decades following a ban on hunting in the 1970s, and as many as 70 or 80 may now inhabit the river. Several of the more impressive specimens – full-grown males may reach 5 metres (16.5 feet) in length – are habituated to the boats of tourists that come to see them. Close views are usually possible, but swimming is definitely off the agenda for humans, as crocodile attacks are all too likely. Equally, care should always be taken when walking along the shore, as the crocodiles frequently bask in warm, sheltered locations near the water.

The chance to watch large crocodiles at close quarters brings many visitors to Daintree, and the park also offers the opportunity to try and see one of Australia's most enigmatic and endangered birds, the Southern Cassowary *Casuarius casuarius johnsonii*. Once widely distributed through

OPPOSITE **The Estuarine Crocodiles or "Salties" of the Daintree River are among the area's most renowned wildlife attractions. The largest reptiles in the world in terms of bulk, they are the top predator across their extensive range, which runs from the Indian subcontinent to here on Australia's east coast. Although capable of taking animals as large as a horse, they tend to live mainly on smaller prey such as fish and crabs.**

LEFT AND LEFT BELOW **The huge number and diversity of frogs and other amphibians are among the highlights of any visit to the Queensland rainforests. Best seen (and heard!) on a night walk after rain has fallen, they include Green Tree Frog *Litoria caerulea* (above) and Graceful Tree Frog *Litoria gracilenta* (below).**

RIGHT **Cassowaries have excellent eyesight and hearing, and the bright colours on their face and neck become more vivid when a bird is excited or alarmed. The precise coloration varies between species and geographical location, but the bare skin around the face invariably gives these birds a decidedly reptilian appearance.**

OPPOSITE **One of the most dramatic lizards found in the Wet Tropics is Boyd's Forest Dragon *Hypsilurus boydii*. The dorsal crest has spines – actually enlarged, flattened scales – running along the length of the body, and the dewlap hanging from the throat is similarly developed. Adults can reach 50 centimetres (20 inches) in length.**

Queensland's rainforests, its only presence in Australia (although it also occurs in New Guinea), the cassowary's population has declined in the face of habitat loss and disturbance. Today as few as 1,000 may survive nationally, with the Cape Tribulation area one of the most likely places to find one, although sightings are generally unpredictable and can never be guaranteed. Named in June 1770 by Captain Cook – "because here began all our Troubles" – after his ship *Endeavour* struck a reef and almost foundered here, Cape Tribulation presents a benign aspect today, a place where luxuriant rainforest tumbles down to reach the beach, which faces out to the Great Barrier Reef offshore.

The world's third-largest bird, Southern Cassowaries are flightless and rely on running to escape predators, although they are also good swimmers and jumpers. They are primitive birds, a relict of the time when Australia and New Guinea were joined by dry land and, more often than not, the first evidence of their presence is a crashing sound as they dash off through the undergrowth to escape danger. Cassowaries are rainforest specialists, and the distinctive bony casque on their head, made of keratin, is used to help hack their way through thick vegetation when on the move, as well as to assist with foraging on the forest floor. Their plumage is made up of coarse, double-stranded feathers, which almost look like hair, and the bare skin of the head and neck become more brightly coloured when the bird is aroused.

Although generally very shy, cassowaries are inquisitive birds and their curiosity sometimes gets the better of them. Some individuals will readily approach human habitation, especially where there are gardens containing fruit, and will even follow people walking along trails in the forest. Cassowaries must be treated with caution at all times, however. With adults (the females are noticeably bigger than the males) standing up to 2 metres (6 feet) tall and weighing as much as 80 kilograms (176 pounds), they are formidable adversaries if cornered and can be aggressive when with young or defending territory. Attacks on humans are well documented – a cassowary will jump and strike out with both legs at the same time, often inflicting serious wounds with the long claws on the inner toes of its feet.

Cassowaries have large home ranges of up to 7 square kilometres (2.5 square miles) and are mainly active at dawn and dusk, usually resting up in sheltered locations during the middle of the

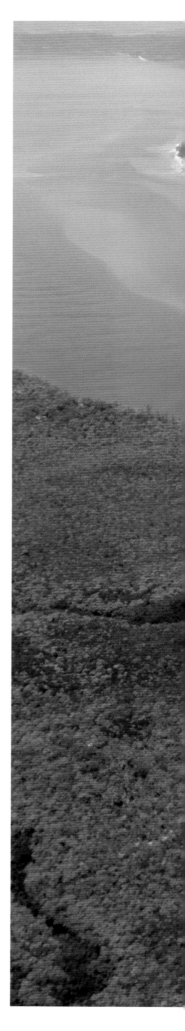

LEFT A cassowary "pizza" of droppings, full of fruit seeds. In this way cassowaries act as important vectors for many species of plant and tree, helping extend the distribution through the forest of what might otherwise be quite localized species.

day. Although generally solitary, during the breeding season – roughly May to November – female birds will wander considerably, passing through the territories of several males in their search for potential mating partners. Unusually, it is the male of the species who prepares the nest site, if that is not too elaborate a description – it is no more than a simple scrape in the ground, lined with grass and leaves, in which the female will lay between three and eight eggs before moving on to the next available male and leaving the previous one to incubate her eggs.

Cassowaries are mainly fruit-eating, plucking fruits from low-hanging branches as well as off the ground, where they will use their feet to sift through the leaf litter. They will also consume invertebrates, fungi, reptiles (including snakes) and amphibians, and have even been seen eating roadkill. They play a critical role in the health of the rainforest, as they are the only large creatures capable of distributing certain species of plants, particularly those containing high levels of toxicity. The cassowaries do this by swallowing the fruit whole and excreting the seeds intact within their dung, which acts as a helpful fertilizer.

In this way they distribute seeds without damaging them in the way that rodents do, for example, and in the Queensland rainforest system they fulfil a role carried out by myriad other creatures in comparable ecosystems elsewhere in the world. Indeed, without such effective dispersal agents, certain tree and plant species would often be restricted to particular confined physical locations, such as gullies, and would be incapable of extending their range. Cassowaries are therefore central to the vegetation diversity of the rainforest.

Habitat loss has had a major impact on cassowary numbers. The Queensland rainforest was formerly much more extensive, but during the twentieth century large areas were cleared to make way for farmland, especially sugarcane plantations. Perhaps as little as 25 per cent of the bird's former habitat survives and, although most of this is now protected, cassowaries still face a range of significant threats. Speeding motorists are the single greatest cause of cassowary deaths in Australia today, while dogs and feral pigs are particularly dangerous to young birds. Disturbance and fragmentation of habitat continue to have a negative impact on the viability of cassowary populations, as well as on other species of rainforest wildlife. Sensitively planned and managed ecotourism in the Cape Tribulation area, and elsewhere in Daintree and the Wet Tropics, is enabling greater numbers of people to experience the rainforest and its specialized flora and fauna. It does, however, raise potentially difficult issues over the extent to which vulnerable creatures like the cassowary can withstand visitor pressure, and whether they will be able to cope with the inevitable interaction with people and the associated infrastructure that such access brings.

RIGHT The estuary of the Daintree River supports globally important tracts of mangroves, which are in turn valuable habitat for a range of wildlife. Over 250 species of fish and crustacean have been recorded here, and birdlife is equally prolific.

9. The Lost World of New Zealand's Stewart Island

Thirty kilometres (18.5 miles) off the southern end of South Island, Stewart Island provides a window into New Zealand's lost past. For here, as virtually nowhere else in the archipelago, it is possible to experience what New Zealand would have looked, and sounded, like before the arrival of humans, and particularly before European colonization began to transform the landscape. The settlers cleared much of the indigenous forest and established European-style agricultural structures in its stead. This transformation clearly had a direct impact on New Zealand's unique native flora and fauna, but more destructive was the havoc wrought by the large variety of creatures the Europeans brought with them, either inadvertently or as deliberate introductions. Rats were among the earliest arrivals, followed by rabbits and then hedgehogs, with ferrets, weasels and stoats all deliberately released later in a misguided attempt to control the rapidly spiralling population of rabbits. Domestic cats were a deadly addition to the mix. The effect on New Zealand's native birds in particular, most of which had evolved in the absence of any natural predators, was catastrophic.

Stewart Island, also known by its Maori name of Rakiura, covers 172,200 hectares (425,500 acres) and is separated from New Zealand's South Island by the Foveaux Strait. This narrow expanse of water saved Stewart from the fate that overtook most of "mainland" New Zealand. Although the Brown Rat *Rattus norvegicus* and domestic cat are present on the island, they have remained largely near the areas of human settlement and, with none of the harmful mustelids introduced, Stewart's flora and fauna largely escaped the ravages of their mainland counterparts. Today much of the island

OPPOSITE **Stewart Island is scenically outstanding, and one of the last places in New Zealand where large tracts of indigenous rainforest survive. One of the most productive sites for native wildlife is Ulva Island, seen here in the middle distance at the heart of Paterson Inlet.**

RIGHT The New Zealand Pigeon is one of the many native birds that are doing well on Stewart Island. It lives primarily on berries, and plays an important role in the healthy condition and essential regeneration of indigenous forest through the dispersal of the fruits and seeds it consumes.

remains undisturbed and less altered from its pre-human condition than probably anywhere else in New Zealand. Dense temperate rainforest covers much (60 per cent) of the island, in many places reaching right down to the water's edge and ringing with a variety of native birdsong.

The character of this magical, near-pristine landscape is defined by the island's oceanic climate, characterized by plentiful rainfall – an average of 1.6 metres (5 feet 2 inches) per annum – spread evenly through the year, and by generally moderate temperatures. These forests are probably the most southerly podocarp forests in the world and were formed after the last glaciation, about 14,000 years ago. As the ice sheets retreated and the climate improved, trees began to establish themselves, their seeds either introduced by birds dispersing from the mainland or carried here on the wind. Today there are over 50 tree and shrub species present in the forests of Stewart Island. Rimu *Dacrydium cupressinum* is very common and the most abundant podocarp emergent (the canopy height at lower elevations is around 30–40 metres/100–130 feet), with Kamahi *Weinmannia racemosa* the dominant canopy hardwood. The Southern Rata or Ironwood *Metrosideros umbellata*, Totara *Podocarpus totara* and Miro *Prumnopitys ferruginea* are also widespread, and species such as Kahikatea *Podocarpus dacrydioides* and Matai *Prumnopitys taxifolia* are plentiful in certain areas. However, there are notable absentees – trees that are present, or even dominant, in areas of similar soil type and climate on the mainland but which did not succeed in establishing themselves before the water flooded what is now the Foveaux Strait. Foremost amongst these are the celery pines *Phyllocladus* spp., and the Silver Beech *Nothofagus menziesii*, which is very common on the mainland but unknown on Stewart.

The island's forest understorey is rich in tree ferns, liverworts and mosses, and the trees themselves support diverse communities of orchids and ferns. Above 300 metres (985 feet) or so, the character of the forest changes in favour of shrub species, a transition also apparent in the more exposed coastal areas, where wind and the effects of salt are major constraints on tree growth. Although some logging of large trees took place near the main settlements in Halfmoon Bay, this activity ceased in the 1930s and the forest one sees today is largely unspoilt – a poignant reminder of a landscape now lost across most of New Zealand. The island has less than 400 human inhabitants, and most of these are now concerned with fishing for oysters and crayfish and, increasingly, with tourism.

Stewart Island is a special place for birds, and for native forest species in particular. Some of the best birding is to be had on Ulva Island in Paterson Inlet, where pest eradication and ensuing

FAR LEFT The lush understorey of native rainforest contains many species of fern, of which over 80 species have been recorded on the island. Among the more impressive are the tree ferns *Cyathea* spp., which are found particularly in wetter areas.

LEFT Once one of the commonest and most conspicuous birds of the native forests on the South Island and on Stewart, the Yellowhead population crashed during the twentieth century. Although habitat loss was partly responsible for this decline, the main cause was predation by introduced Stoats.

habitat recovery made possible the reintroduction of "lost" species such as Stewart Island Robin *Petroica rakiura*, South Island Saddleback *Philesturnus carunculatus carunculatus*, Yellowhead *Mohua ochrocephala* and Rifleman *Acanthisitta chloris*. These are all thriving there, alongside other indigenous birds like Bellbird *Anthornis melanura*, Tui *Prosthemadera novaeseelandiae*, Kaka *Nestor meridionalis*, New Zealand Pigeon *Hemiphaga novaeseelandiae*, Red-fronted Parakeet *Cyanoramphus novaezelandiae*, and Yellow-fronted Parakeet *Cyanoramphus auriceps*, all of which also occur on the main island.

However, it is for two particular species of bird that Stewart Island is most well known: the highly endangered Kakapo *Strigops habroptilus* and the Stewart Island Brown Kiwi or Southern Tokoeka *Apteryx australis lawryi*. The former is no longer found on Stewart Island itself, whilst the latter draws thousands of birders here every year.

The world's only flightless parrot, the enigmatic Kakapo is also the heaviest parrot species, weighing 2–4 kilograms (4–9 pounds) and the only species of the family that is essentially terrestrial and nocturnal. During the day it shelters in thick undergrowth, burrows or crevices in rocks, emerging at dusk to search for food, mostly fruit, shoots and seeds, which it locates partly thanks to its strong sense of smell. Locomotion is by means of its strong legs, on which it moves in a distinctive jog along what become well-worn paths, often scrambling up into trees in search of food (they are excellent climbers). The Kakapo's flightlessness is an evolutionary response to the absence of any native terrestrial predators in New Zealand and, like the kiwis, it has evolved to occupy the ecological niche normally filled by mammals (of which there are only three indigenous species in New Zealand – all bats).

Although the Kakapo was once fairly widely distributed on both the North and South Islands, as well as on Stewart, its inability to fly – and its habit of "freezing" and relying on its cryptic

plumage for camouflage when confronted by a threat – rendered it largely defenceless in the face of introduced predators such as cats and mustelids. Like much of New Zealand's native wildlife, the Kakapo's population plummeted in direct response to the spread of these animals, a process exacerbated by hunting and forest clearance. By the mid-1970s the species appeared effectively doomed, with only 14 surviving birds – all of them male.

Then, in 1977, an extraordinary discovery was made on Stewart Island – a hitherto unknown but substantial population of Kakapos. However, these were being killed by feral cats at such a rate that they were likely to be completely extirpated within a few years. Although the cats were subsequently controlled they could not be entirely wiped out, so the decision was therefore taken to capture the 40 surviving Kakapos and evacuate them to predator-free offshore islands where they would be secure. One such location is Codfish Island, just three kilometres (1.8 miles) from Stewart. Here a population of Kakapos is carefully protected and monitored, and numbers are increasing slowly. At the time of writing (March 2008) the total world population was just 92 birds; the species is effectively extinct in the wild, with no known extant natural population, although it is just possible that one or two individuals may survive in remote areas of South Island.

While the Kakapo can no longer be seen on Stewart Island itself, the island is *the* place to see New Zealand's iconic endemic bird, the kiwi, in the wild. There are at least four species of kiwi (debate continues over exactly how many species and sub-species can safely be assigned) across the North and South Islands and on offshore islands like Stewart, but all populations have been hard pressed by non-native predators. Conservation programmes are helping stem the decline nationally, and the Stewart Island population of some 20,000 birds is one of the largest and most stable in the country. Notorious for their shy and retiring nature, kiwis mostly emerge from their burrows only under cover of darkness, behaviour that has developed in response to the presence of diurnal

BELOW The Kakapo's largely nocturnal habits, and a facial disc of feathers that give it a decidedly owl-like cast, are reflected in its alternative common names of Night Parrot and Owl Parrot. The whiskers or *vibrissae* around the bird's beak serve as antennae, enabling it to detect potential obstacles when shuffling along the ground, head-down.

ABOVE **Kiwis are distinctly unbirdlike. The absence of interlocking barbules on their feathers gives their plumage a fur-like texture, and their rolling, rather mechanical gait is akin to that of a mammal. Whereas elsewhere in New Zealand they are usually seen on their own or in pairs, on Stewart it is not uncommon to see small groups foraging together – often two parents with a youngster.**

predators. Interestingly on Stewart – where such predators are either absent or fewer in number – kiwis are less strictly nocturnal than elsewhere and can on occasion be seen out and about during the day. While some live inside the forest proper, most prefer the tussocky grassland and scrub of the coastal strip, particularly around Mason Bay on the west coast, where they can even be seen foraging on the beach. Evenings are the best time to spot them.

The rainforests of Stewart Island, and especially that on Ulva Island, are a precious survival. Pest control and conservation work, on both the main island and the offshore islets, are helping to secure the future of the forest and its wildlife – the understorey and the canopy of the forest are still affected by the browsing of introduced White-tailed Deer *Odocoileus virginianus* and Brush-tailed Possums *Trichosurus vulpecula*, for example, and feral cats continue to predate kiwis and other native species. Indeed, their continued presence is likely to preclude the early reintroduction of the Kakapo. Meanwhile, the growing number of humans visiting the island is raising interesting issues over sustainability and the impact too many visitors might have on the very atmosphere they come to savour. For the time being at least, Stewart remains an iconic place, a glimpse of primeval New Zealand and a reminder of what might be regained on other islands if their predators can be removed and their forests recovered. This is surely worth doing, if only to give more New Zealanders the chance to be thrilled by a dawn chorus delivered by their country's native birds rather than by introduced European species.

OPPOSITE **In many parts of Stewart Island native forest reaches right down to the seashore, giving the unspoilt and "primeval" feel that many visitors here value greatly. In addition to its rainforest landscapes and associated wildlife, Stewart is also important for marine life and seabirds, including penguins. Eighty-five per cent of the island was gazetted as Rakiura National Park in 2002.**

10. The Mighty Sepik River, Papua New Guinea

The world's second-largest island, New Guinea contains some of the planet's last great wildernesses. Covering some 462,000 square kilometres (179,000 square miles), it has a huge diversity of habitats, from mangrove forest through tropical lowland rainforest, swamp forest and savannah grassland to montane rainforest, cloudforest, moorland and alpine scree. Such a wide variety of ecosystems invariably fosters high levels of biodiversity, yet much of the island remains *terra incognita* to biologists. Every scientific expedition to the more remote regions turns up surprises, and it is certain that there are whole rafts of species yet to be brought to the attention of science. Ethnographically, New Guinea is outstanding. Its indigenous people, many of whom still follow highly traditional lives away from the trappings of "modern" society, maintain a complex culture that is inextricably linked to their environment and the wildlife it supports. This close association is symbolized in many of their traditional rituals.

The Sepik is New Guinea's Amazon or Congo, the island's longest and culturally most important river. From its source in the central highlands of Papua New Guinea it winds for 1,126 kilometres (700 miles) to its point of entry into the Bismarck Sea. As the coastline here shelves immediately into deep water, the Sepik has no estuary or delta, the silt-filled river simply discharging into

BELOW The Sepik River winds through a large part of north-west Papua New Guinea. Many of its deep meanders have evolved into oxbow lakes (see the example centre left in this aerial shot), which are excellent places for waterbirds.

OPPOSITE Quite unmistakable, the Palm Cockatoo *Probosciger aterrimus* is the only all-black member of its family. This species is generally scarce and rather localized, but can be found in reasonable numbers in the gallery forest along stretches of the Sepik.

the open ocean in a great brown stain that can be seen up to 50 kilometres (30 miles) out to sea. En route across the north-west of Papua New Guinea, it passes through a floodplain up to 70 kilometres (40 miles) wide in places, the course of the river characterized by deep meanders and a large number of oxbow lakes. The largest of these, Chambri Lake, is the second-biggest inland body of water on the whole island.

Much of the Sepik basin, into which a large number of associated smaller rivers and tributaries flow, is undisturbed, and collectively the basin represents the largest unpolluted freshwater system in New Guinea. Although there has been some logging in more accessible places along the lower Sepik, where rubber and cocoa plantations have been established, most of the natural habitats in the basin are in largely pristine condition. There are vast tracts of swamp and riparian forest, much of which is periodically flooded, sometimes for months on end. On drier land, primary lowland rainforest extends up to the Hunstein Range, part of the central cordillera that runs across New Guinea, with the area around the lower Niksek (a tributary of the Sepik) forming the largest protected expanse of rainforest on the island.

The river complex itself is home to at least 75 species of indigenous freshwater fish, as well as several introduced species (including tilapia, now an important component in the local diet). It also supports important populations of two species of crocodile, the Estuarine or Saltwater *Crocodylus porosus* and the much smaller New Guinea Freshwater *C. novaeguineae*. By the 1980s the populations of both had declined significantly, owing to excessive commercial exploitation (hunting for hides, and

BELOW **Travelling by boat on the river is undoubtedly one of the most rewarding ways of exploring this often inaccessible region of New Guinea. Many species of bird and animal favour the forest edge, and non-motorized craft offer the opportunity to make a close approach. Guided boat trips for tourists are therefore an increasing economic opportunity for local people as rainforest ecotourism expands here.**

RIGHT New Guinea is the world's headquarters for tree kangaroos, although two species also occur in northern Australia. Most are found in montane rainforests, but some species – such as Goodfellow's Tree Kangaroo *Dendrolagus goodfellowi*, shown here – are mainly restricted to lowland areas, such as the Sepik basin.

the taking of eggs for food) and, in the case of the freshwater species, the disturbance of nursery areas on the floating mats of vegetation that are a characteristic feature of sections of the river. However, a highly successful management scheme aimed at establishing and maintaining the conditions required by crocodiles has helped their numbers recover to the point at which an annual "harvest" is both feasible and sustainable. Crocodiles (known locally as *puk puk*) play an important role in Sepik culture, embodying strength and power. As part of a boy's passage to manhood, his back is cut ritualistically, the resultant scarification designed to resemble the pattern of ridges on a crocodile's back; the idea being that he has been swallowed by a crocodile and then emerges as a man. Wooden carvings in the Sepik region are characterized by a high incidence of crocodile-inspired motifs.

As in much of New Guinea, the flora and fauna of the Sepik basin are imperfectly researched and understood. As many as 120 of the island's 200 mammal species are present here, including a wide range of marsupials, among them tree kangaroos. Ten of the world's twelve species of tree kangaroo occur in New Guinea's rainforests, and the absence on the island (and in Australasia generally) of primates may explain why kangaroos evolved to fill a vacant arboreal niche. Armed with long claws to assist with climbing and scrambling through the canopy, tree kangaroos are physically quite different from their terrestrial cousins, their hindlegs less well developed and more in proportion with their powerfully built forelegs. Nonetheless, they are prodigious jumpers,

The Victoria Crowned Pigeon is one of the most dramatic of all forest birds, yet despite its size it can be difficult to see well in the dense understorey. The species is monogamous, mating for life and rearing just one young each year, factors which make it difficult for it to recover its numbers in places where hunting pressure is particularly intense.

BELOW The Sepik basin is home to a variety of parrots, including the Dusky Lory *Pseudeos fuscata*, shown here. Parrots have suffered worldwide for many decades through excessive collection for the live-bird trade. As a result many species are now endangered, with some already driven to the point of extinction and several others so depleted in the wild that their future will depend on captive breeding programmes.

capable of leaping up to 9 or 10 metres (30 feet) from trees down onto the ground. As with other kangaroos and wallabies, they use their tail to assist with balance.

Tree kangaroos live in small family groups and, despite their name, are far from being exclusively arboreal. Where unmolested, they will often descend to ground level, foraging for fallen fruit and nuts in particular, but they move awkwardly and slowly on the forest floor, shuffling about in small hops. In such situations they are vulnerable to humans, their only predator, and in certain areas excessive hunting has reduced their numbers or totally extirpated certain populations. Habitat loss, caused by logging activity and other forms of disturbance, is also an increasing threat.

The abundant birdlife of the Sepik basin – probably in excess of 300 species – includes an important range of waterbirds, found along the river and its associated wetlands, as well as many species of parrot and some of New Guinea's flagship rainforest species. These include two of the island's three species of cassowary, Dwarf *Casuarius bennetti* and Northern *C. unappendiculatus*, both traditionally hunted for food by local people, and the world's largest pigeon, the Victoria Crowned Pigeon *Goura victoria*. Weighing up to 2.5 kilograms (5.5 pounds) and as much as 74 centimetres (29 inches) long, this impressive bird is especially noted for its extravagant headgear, a crest of lacy feathers that form a fan when erected and spread out. The pigeon's largely terrestrial habits and confiding nature make it a popular and easy quarry for hunters, who value it both for its plumage and its tender meat. Often found in small groups, this species favours lowland and swamp forest and, although numbers may be declining, it remains tolerably common in parts of the Sepik basin.

This area also has records of the endemic New Guinea Harpy-Eagle *Harpyopsis novaeguineae*, one of the most impressive but least-known large raptors in the world. Restricted to the island's rainforests, this elusive species is unlike most large birds of prey in that it is curiously sedentary by nature. Rather than hunt primarily by soaring above the canopy, it appears to prefer to sit high *in* the canopy and then take short glides – or even walk or hop – towards its prey. Remarkably inconspicuous for such a large bird (adults reach up to 90 centimetres/35 inches in length), it feeds mainly on small mammals but has also been recorded taking reptiles and, on occasion, other birds. Little data exists on its population status, but it is not common anywhere and is under pressure across much of its range from both habitat loss and from hunters – its feathers are highly prized for ceremonial use.

Approximately half a million people live along the Sepik, and most still derive their livelihood from the river and surrounding forest. The use in traditional ceremonial dress of feathers – especially those of birds of paradise – is an integral part of local culture and *per se* appears to have had little impact historically on overall bird populations. However, when coupled with habitat loss – an increasing problem in many parts of New Guinea – it is clear that hunting (whether for plumage, hides or meat) can have an adverse effect at a local level. In some areas of the island, especially sought-after species have become scarce or retreated to more inaccessible tracts of forest.

BELOW Butterflies and moths in New Guinea remain a largely unknown quantity, with many new species being described every year. The world's largest moth, the Atlas Moth *Attacus atlas*, is widespread across much of the island and quite unmistakable.

The impact of hunting becomes a particular issue when forests are fragmented to the point at which isolated pockets of wildlife are unable to be replenished, either numerically or genetically, from other centres of population.

Sepik art and architecture are among the most iconic emblems of indigenous New Guinea culture, the tribes of this region renowned particularly for the character and quality of their woodcarving and for their celebrated village architecture. Sepik art is bound up with ritual magic and myth, epitomized in the celebrated village spirit houses or *haus tambarans*, which are traditionally decorated with masks and other carvings. The fascinating human dimension of the Sepik basin, combined with the unspoilt character of much of the local forest environment, make the region a compellingly strong candidate for the continued development of limited ecotourism.

Community involvement through the provision of homestays and guiding may help local people adjust more satisfactorily to the outside influences that are increasingly impinging on their traditional way of life. Particular threats to the rainforest include the spectres of opencast mining and large-scale logging. So far the remarkable island of New Guinea has escaped the worst excesses of environmental degradation as seen elsewhere in the Asia-Pacific region. Yet approximately 80 per cent of Papua New Guinea's lowland forest has already been granted to forestry concessions – the next decade or so will be the acid test of whether one of the world's last great rainforests can survive.

LEFT The tribes of the Sepik basin have traditionally lived in close physical and spiritual harmony with the river and the rainforest environment. As the modern world increasingly intrudes into their way of life, the challenge for them will be to find new roles that enable them to retain these links whilst also benefiting economically.

RIGHT The East Sepik region is noted for its indigenous architecture, and in particular for its *haus tambarans*. These highly distinctive spirit houses sit at the apex of local tribal life, serving as meeting-places and as venues for ceremonies, rituals and initiations.

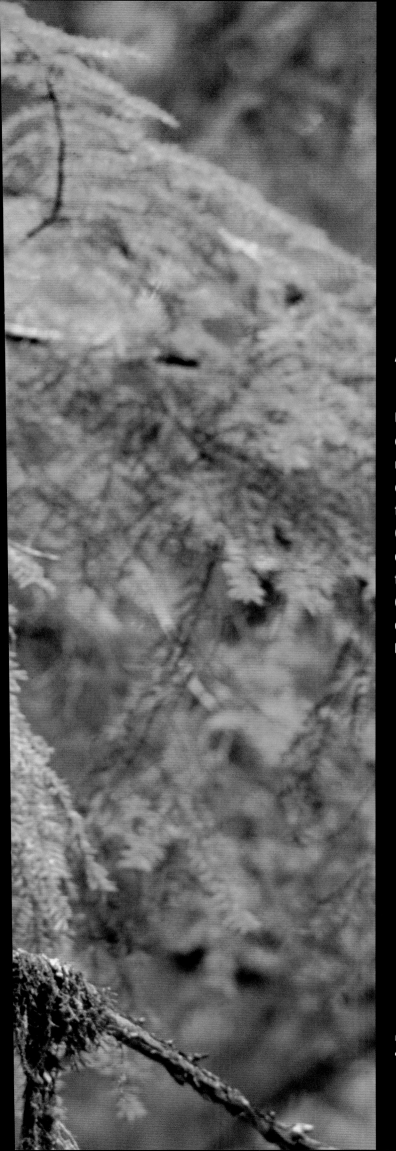

NORTH AMERICA

Home to the world's largest surviving tracts of temperate rainforest, the north-western coasts of North America offer precisely the conditions required by rainforest plants: high levels of rainfall and generally equable conditions with no real temperature extremes. A dense forest composed of hemlock, spruce, fir and cedar once ran along the coastline in an unbroken belt from Alaska through British Columbia south to Washington State, Oregon and into northern California. Today this once great expanse of trees – home to bears, wolves and a wealth of other wildlife – is a series of largely disconnected fragments, a victim of logging and other forms of exploitation. However, some tracts of old-growth forest do survive, mostly along Canada's so-called Raincoast, and these are the focal point of a move to stem the tide of destruction and raise awareness of the value of these unique rainforests, which are every bit as precious as their tropical counterparts.

LEFT An icon of North America's temperate rainforests, the Northern Spotted Owl was the focus of a bitter dispute between conservationists and the timber industry during the closing decades of the twentieth century.

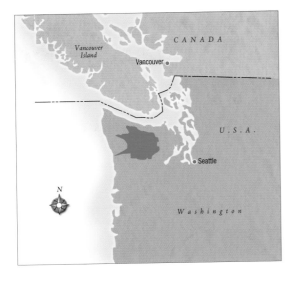

11. America's Greatest Rainforest: Olympic National Park

The west-facing valleys of the Olympic Peninsula in the USA's Washington State are among the wettest places in North America. Some of them receive a phenomenal 4.5 metres (15 feet) of rain every year, as prevailing winds drive moisture off the Pacific Ocean and then up against the Olympic Mountains, the cooling process producing clouds full of rain. Although about three-quarters of the rainfall occurs outside the summer months, humidity levels are maintained at that time by a high incidence of fog. The mountains protect the littoral from the temperature extremes of the interior, providing perfect conditions for the growth of temperate rainforest. This is a primeval landscape, dominated by coniferous trees such as Sitka Spruce *Picea sitchensis*, Western Hemlock *Tsuga heterophylla*, Douglas Fir *Pseudotsuga menziesii* and Western Red Cedar *Thuja plicata*, but with a supporting cast of deciduous species including Bigleaf Maple *Acer macrophyllum* and Black Cottonwood *Populus trichocarpa* in drier locations. The Sitka Spruce is the iconic tree of the forest; the most mature individuals are several centuries' old, reach up to 90 metres (300 feet) tall and have a trunk circumference of as much as 18 metres (60 feet).

Temperate rainforests are every bit as lush as their tropical counterparts. The most striking characteristic of those in the Pacific Northwest is the profusion of epiphytic species, notably mosses, lichens and ferns. These cloak the trees as well as the forest floor, over which they form a deep carpet of moist greenery alongside ground-cover species such as Oregon Wood-sorrel *Oxalis oregana*. Thereby denied easy access to the soil beneath, tree seedlings germinate most effectively on the fallen trunks of their ancestors, which litter the forest floor. Once established in a damp niche in the rotting wood, a seedling will send down roots below. When the trunk – known as a nurse log – eventually rots away, the youngsters remain slightly above ground level on stilt-like roots and often with several of them growing in a line along the axis of the old trunk, in a row known as a colonnade. These colonnades are a characteristic feature of the forest here.

OPPOSITE **Moose occur widely in the temperate rainforests of the Pacific Northwest but at generally low densities. They usually avoid thick vegetation, preferring more open terrain near lakes or rivers, where they feed extensively on aquatic vegetation. Only the males have antlers, which are shed every autumn. A new set grows in spring, initially covered in a layer of skin known as velvet.**

RIGHT **A typical streamside habitat in the Hoh Valley, one of the best-preserved tracts of temperate rainforest in Olympic National Park. The forest floor is home to complex communities of micro-organisms, as well as a wide variety of plants and invertebrates. Diversity increases when in immediate proximity to water.**

Surrounded by sea on three sides and including 118 kilometres (73 miles) of dramatic coastline, as well as the ice-capped peaks around Mount Olympus, Olympic National Park was established in 1938 to protect the largest remaining contiguous tract of temperate rainforest in the United States. Seven decades later, with the park a World Heritage Site and Biosphere Reserve, the foresight behind the decision to safeguard this precious resource is all too apparent. Almost all other areas of pristine rainforest in the United States have been systematically logged, with only fragments remaining of the great North American rainforests that once stretched in an unbroken sweep from south-eastern Alaska to southern Oregon. Inside the park, which covers 3,600 square kilometres (1,400 square miles), the forests found along the valleys of the rivers Bogahiel, Hoh, Queets and Quinault are among the best examples of what has been destroyed elsewhere.

Although the temperate rainforests of the Pacific Northwest have much lower levels of biodiversity than their tropical equivalents, they support a range of specialized wildlife. Exactly how important they are ecologically only really came to public attention in the 1980s and '90s, as a result of a major confrontation between conservationists and the logging industry over the plight of a bird that was to become an iconic symbol for some and a focus of hate for others.

The Northern Spotted Owl *Strix occidentalis caurina* is the most northern of three subspecies and ranges from the extreme south of British Columbia in Canada (where only a few pairs remain) south to northern California. Highly sedentary, the species is heavily dependent on old-growth forest and by the mid-twentieth century it was clear that its numbers and distribution were being severely affected by the clear-felling of that habitat across much of its range. Research revealed that many pairs of owls were failing to breed every year and that chicks were suffering a high mortality rate, especially at the dispersal stage when they were leaving their natal area to try to establish a territory of their own in ever dwindling tracts of suitable habitat.

As if that were not enough, the creation of more open habitats within the forest environment – a direct outcome of logging activity – had favoured an invasion of Barred Owl *Strix varia*, which extended its range from the Midwest, directly competing with the Spotteds and even predating them.

With the Northern Spotted Owl under severe pressure, conservationists campaigned successfully for both it and its habitat to be given effective and immediate protection. It was duly listed as a threatened species under the Endangered Species Act, but the most controversial measure was a court order of 1991 instructing the cessation of logging in areas of prime owl habitat on federal land. The forestry industry was outraged, predicting a big loss of jobs and a supply crisis

ABOVE **A clear-felled area of temperate rainforest, a depressing sight for anyone interested in wildlife or the environment. The plundering of the west coast forests became a regional political issue during the late-twentieth century and, while conservation criteria are given greater emphasis today than previously, logging still continues at some sensitive sites.**

RIGHT **A Northern Spotted Owl sitting on branches draped in the hanging moss *Selaginella oregana*. Along with various other species of moss, as well as liverworts, lichens, ferns and other epiphytes, Selaginella forms an arboreal plant community that accounts for the majority of the biomass in temperate rainforests.**

LEFT **Several thousand Roosevelt Elk live in Olympic National Park. They are at their most obvious and dramatic during the autumn, the season of the annual rut, when the bulls challenge each other for access to females. Bellowing and fighting are the order of the day, and the mature bulls require all their strength and stamina to see off younger rivals.**

caused by the fall in the timber harvest, now that most federal land was off limits. Loggers and sawmill owners campaigned vociferously against the decision, even to the extent of publicly burning effigies of the owl, but the conservation measures remained in place and are still regarded by some as the death knell of the local timber industry.

Today it is estimated that there may be as many as 3,200 pairs of Northern Spotted Owls across the western United States, and the Olympic National Park supports a healthy population. Yet the species is still not secure. The continuation of logging on privately owned land doubtless reduces available habitat (a nesting pair of Spotted Owls requires a territory of 800–1,600 hectares/2,000–4,000 acres, with a preference for Douglas Fir), and the issue of competition with the Barred Owl continues to have an impact.

One of the outcomes of the 1990s controversy was a wider understanding that the Spotted Owl serves as an indicator species for the entire temperate rainforest ecosystem. Greater appreciation of the unique qualities of the forest, and of the particular character of its flora and fauna, has followed, and in this respect Olympic National Park acts as showcase for the wider rainforest environment. Some 300 species of bird and 50 of mammal live here, one of the most important historically being the Roosevelt Elk *Cervus canadensis roosevelti*, which played a seminal role in the establishment of the park. In the early years of the twentieth century this species was reduced by overhunting to the brink of extinction, with the Olympic area supporting the largest remaining population. It was the personal interest of President Theodore Roosevelt, a keen sportsman, that helped secure their protection, with the declaration in 1909 of the Mount Olympus National Monument, chosen specifically to protect the elk's summer calving grounds. This decision proved to be the prelude to eventual national park status.

With mature males (usually known as bulls) regularly weighing in at over 400 kilograms (880 pounds), the elk is the second heaviest mammal in the world after the Moose *Alces alces*. A temperate rainforest inhabitant for much of the year, it moves to higher altitudes during the summer to take advantage of the plentiful seasonal grazing. Following the local extinction of the Grey Wolf *Canis lupus* before the park's establishment, the elk's two main predators have been the Black Bear *Ursus americanus* and the Puma or Cougar *Puma concolor*. Once under intense pressure across much of its United States' range, the Puma has recovered its numbers in recent years and is now reasonably common in the park, albeit rarely seen. Mature males can be up to 2.5 metres (8.5 feet) in length, and although usually lighter in weight than their prey, are certainly capable of bringing down a mature elk. However, attacks on younger or sickly individuals are more usual, with the Columbia Black-tailed Deer *Odocoileus hemionus columbianus* also a regular prey species.

RIGHT **The young shoots of Common Horsetail *Equisetum arvense* are a common springtime sight in the forest. The forest floor is densely carpeted with mosses, lichens, ferns and ground-cover plants, so special adaptations are required to break through to the light. The horsetail has a vigorous network of rhizomes to help ensure it competes successfully.**

A recent conservation story in the park has been the reintroduction of the Fisher *Martes pennanti*, a member of the weasel family. The Fisher was virtually eradicated from Washington State during the twentieth century as a result of excessive trapping and habitat loss. In January 2008 eleven animals were released in Olympic National Park, the first batch in a projected total of some one hundred animals to be introduced here over a three-year period. Fishers are not especially partial to fish – their English name is thought to originate from the French word *fichet*, meaning the pelt of a polecat – but they are highly successful omnivorous predators and appear to specialize in killing porcupines, the only North American carnivore to do so regularly.

The unexpected character of the temperate rainforest environment, and of the park generally, is highlighted no more effectively than by the case of the Marbled Murrelet *Brachyramphus marmoratus*. A member of the essentially coast- and oceanic-dwelling auk family, this species is remarkable in that, instead of nesting colonially near the sea like other members of its family, it breeds in old-growth forest as far as 80 kilometres (50 miles) inland. The lone female lays her single egg on a bed of lichen or moss on a large branch some 20–40 metres (65–130 feet) high in the canopy (although ground-nesting has been recorded in Alaska), and once the chick is fledged it is left to make its own way to the sea. It does this by flying direct, and non-stop, to the ocean, an extraordinary journey by any standards. The murrelet's unusual choice of breeding location had remained a mystery until a chance discovery in 1974, and its breeding range remains imperfectly understood. What is known, however, is that the species suffers a high mortality rate during the "egg to sea" phase, and is very vulnerable to disturbance on its nesting grounds. Its uncertain situation serves to underline how important and fragile the temperate rainforest environment is.

RIGHT Although good numbers of Cougars or Mountain Lions (also known as Pumas) live in the park, they are highly elusive and hardly ever seen, even by park rangers. Whilst they are generally wary of humans, attacks on hikers are not unknown and care should always be taken when walking in likely cougar country.

LEFT A reintroduction programme was the only option for returning the Fisher to its former haunts in the Olympic Peninsula. Overhunting had reduced this species to the very brink of extinction here, if not wiped it out completely, so it was highly unlikely ever to make a return without human assistance.

LEFT The bizarre life cycle of the Marbled Murrelet, a maritime bird which nests inland, somehow symbolizes the special character of the temperate rainforest. The unity of the sea and the forest, and the links between the two, are essential components of this remarkable ecosystem.

12. The Great Bear Rainforest of British Columbia, Canada

The dramatic so-called "Raincoast" of British Columbia in western Canada is one of the world's last great wildernesses. This is a beautiful and rugged landscape, where mountains cascade down to a coastline interlaced by hundreds of inlets, estuaries and islands. It remains largely remote and often inaccessible country, drenched in mist and rain on many days each year, and supporting what is the most important surviving tract of old-growth temperate rainforest in North America: the Great Bear Rainforest. Covering almost 70,000 square kilometres (27,000 square miles) and stretching for 500 kilometres (310 miles) from the southern tip of the Alaskan Panhandle south to a point on the mainland broadly opposite the northern end of Vancouver Island, this forest is one of the continent's most important ecosystems. It is also home to some of the oldest and largest trees found anywhere; many of them are several centuries old, with more ancient specimens certainly in excess of 1,000 years in age and some perhaps as much as 1,500 years old. All this in an area once known to the logging industry as the "Mid-Coast Timber Supply Area".

The Great Bear Rainforest was established as a formal entity in 2006, when a complex land-use agreement was brokered between the British Columbia government, First Nations groups

OPPOSITE **Western Canada's Raincoast is a complex network of inlets and estuaries interfaced with an archipelago of many hundreds of islands. This sensitive environment is highly vulnerable to disturbance.**

BELOW **The cathedral-like effect of the coastal rainforest makes for scenery of the utmost drama. Huge trees tower above river mouths and inlets, backed by precipitous slopes rising into the mist. Some of North America's best wildlife-watching is possible here, with a high density of bears and one of the world's most interesting wolf populations.**

(representing Canada's indigenous peoples), conservationists and the logging industry. By the 1990s the rate at which old growth forest was being clear-felled, and the impact of such activity on the region's still imperfectly understood ecosystems, had prompted international concern. The agreement sought to safeguard important sections of the rainforest through a series of nature conservancies and protected areas (covering roughly one-third of its total extent), and was aimed at protecting the region's ecological and cultural significance while also satisfying the demands of the logging and timber industries. In particular, it was intended that these measures would ensure the future of iconic wildlife species such as the forest's important populations of bears (both Black *Ursus americanus* and Grizzly *U. arctos horribilis*) and its unique coastal-dwelling packs of Grey Wolf *Canis lupus*.

The forest is composed mainly of classic West Coast tree species such as Western Hemlock *Tsuga heterophylla*, Sitka Spruce *Picea sitchensis*, Western Red Cedar *Thuja plicata* and Pacific Silver Fir *Abies amabilis*, with some Douglas Fir *Pseudotsuga menziesii*. Although general levels of biodiversity are typically lower in temperate rainforests than in their tropical counterparts, in terms of overall biomass – the total weight of living organisms – the temperate zone rainforests may have the edge. Certainly the terrestrial and marine ecosystems in this region enjoy a close and dynamic relationship, with the forest sustained by moisture generated by the proximity of the ocean and by the nutrient sources that the sea brings to the land. Foremost among these are the vast numbers of salmon *Onchorynchus* spp., six species of which come to spawn here each year. It is estimated that over 2,500 known salmon runs are located along the Great Bear

OPPOSITE The area's population of salmon makes up a substantial percentage of the annual bear diet, but some bears are more accomplished at fishing than others. The less competent sometimes develop a skill of their own, whereby they wait for another, smaller, bear to catch something and then steal it from them.

BELOW Salmon are central to the Raincoast ecosystem. Through vectors such as birds, bears and wolves, the nutrients they contain are distributed throughout the rainforest, enriching it in a way that defines its character and is the bedrock of its biodiversity. Old-growth forests are essential to maintaining the stability of the stream environments in which the salmon spawn.

Rainforest coast, one of the last great concentrations in North America and attracting as much as 20 per cent of the world's wild salmon. The streams and rivers that snake their way inland are the corridors by which one of the forest's main sources of nutrients arrives to replenish the soil and vegetation, transferred by vectors such as terrestrial carnivores.

As the salmon pile in, the estuaries and other waterways become the focus of hungry predators. Large numbers of bears gather to take advantage of the influx – salmon may provide as much as 95 per cent of their autumn diet, after the bears have spent the spring and early summer feeding primarily on sedges and other plants, supplemented by crabs and shellfish. Wolves also actively hunt the fish, and a host of scavenging birds, such as Bald Eagle *Haliaeetus leucocephalus*, Common Raven *Corvus corax*, and gulls *Larus* spp. are attracted by the rich pickings, especially as the salmon die after spawning, their carcases littering the shallows. Most importantly, however, the bears and wolves carry the salmon that they have caught well into the forest, where the decomposing remains of what they do not consume support a range of scavenging vertebrates, invertebrates and birds, as well as enriching the soil and thereby feeding the trees and other plants. In this way the bears and wolves play a critical role in distributing ocean-generated nutrients within the forest, a chain that is so distinct and so thorough that the isotopic (or chemical) signatures of salmon have been detected in the leaves of the trees.

BELOW **Bald Eagles declined markedly during the mid-twentieth century as a result of persecution and the use of pesticides such as DDT. Numbers have recovered well following protection and the banning of harmful chemicals, and today the Raincoast and adjacent coastline in Alaska and Washington State are the main strongholds of this magnificent bird.**

OPPOSITE **A mother "Spirit" Bear with her two cubs. In this instance the father clearly did not carry the Spirit gene, as the offspring are the traditional dark brown/black colour. The white or, more accurately, cream-coloured bears have always been scarce, their rarity value doubtless helping to contribute to the high status conferred on them by the region's indigenous people.**

RIGHT Raincoast wolves are elusive and difficult to study at close quarters. Encounters are largely a matter of luck, and often take place when the wolves are scavenging on the coastal flats, or grassy areas next to water.

BELOW The sheer volume of living organisms in the rainforest can be quite literally overwhelming. Fallen trees and stumps are smothered in a dense carpet of life, which, with the canopy structure above, collectively forms a biomass that is greater in temperate rainforests than in their equatorial counterparts.

LEFT Some 75 per cent of the diet of the so-called "outer-coast" wolves comes from marine sources, mainly salmon. For "inner-coast" wolves the figure is more like 50 per cent, as they take more mammals such as Moose and deer.

The rainforest's population of Grizzly Bears includes the most southerly Pacific coastal-dwelling representatives of their species. The region is also celebrated for its Black Bears, particularly the local subspecies *Ursus americanus kermodei*, the Kermode Bear. This population is notable for the high incidence of white – or, rather, cream-coloured – individuals, known as "Spirit" Bears. Although this recessive genetic trait has been recorded occasionally from elsewhere in the Black Bear's extensive North American distribution, only on this stretch of the Canadian coast are white bears present in such numbers. Even so, there are probably fewer than 150 in total.

The white bears are a prominent feature in the historical mythology of the indigenous First Nation people, but they were not described to science until 1905 and exactly how the genetic variation works is still unclear. It is not a form of albinism – the skin and eyes of the white bears are dark – and may be partly explained by the relative isolation in which the Kermode subspecies has evolved, separated from other populations of Black Bear by the physical configuration of its habitat – there seems to be a higher incidence of white bears on some of the islands, for example. The white phase requires the recessive gene to be passed on by both parents, so a pair of black Kermode Bears may produce white offspring, and two white Kermode Bears may have black young.

ABOVE **The particular nature of the terrain along the Raincoast dictates the behaviour of the local wolves. Highly peripatetic, they are good swimmers and regularly move between islands in search of food and secure denning sites. Deer and bears are equally capable of crossing the smaller inlets and channels.**

Bears notwithstanding, the temperate rainforest's top predator is arguably the Grey Wolf. Although the wolves of the Raincoast are slightly smaller than their inland cousins, and rather leaner, they will on occasion hunt and kill bears, especially Black Bears. Evidence suggests that they tackle bears more readily than do wolves in other types of habitat, a possible reflection of the high local Black Bear density and competition over salmon. The wolves usually favour smaller and less dangerous prey, feeding mainly on Sitka Black-tailed Deer *Odocoileus hemionus sitkensis*, but what makes them particularly different from inland wolves is the fact that their diet is critically supplemented on a seasonal basis by salmon. The coastal wolves are good swimmers and very skilled at fishing, often wading into rivers and estuaries and grabbing the fish in their jaws. They have even been observed chasing their prey into the shallows, where it can be caught more easily, and are especially partial to the brains of salmon, usually tearing the head off and leaving the rest of the carcase.

The rainforest wolves are extremely elusive, and difficult to locate and observe. Many of them lead a peripatetic form of "island life", often commuting between islands, especially when prey is in short supply in particular locations. Much of our understanding about their ecology comes from examination of their scat, the most readily accessible source of information about their diet and behaviour, although analysis of their hair has also proved useful. The evidence suggests they are genetically different from other wolves, which, together with their ecological distinctiveness, has encouraged scientists to argue that these enigmatic animals merit special protection.

Sadly, the wolf is under threat now. Wolves are still treated as vermin in much of British Columbia, which has no protective legislation for endangered species. Certain areas of the province implement predator control programmes designed to eradicate wolves, or at least sterilize them. There are few accurate figures on how many are killed. The nature of the coastal population – scattered widely, with many living on islands – makes them vulnerable, but the inaccessible terrain in which they live has traditionally been to their advantage.

Outside the protected areas, trophy and sport hunters kill not only wolves but bears too, and the rainforest itself has continued to suffer from delays in implementing the agreements signed in 2006 and from continued wrangling between the various interested parties, not least the loggers and environmentalists. Industrial logging has left significant swathes of unprotected but still wildlife-rich forest little more than a wasteland of leached soil and rotting stumps, and the impact such destruction has on local habitats – and on the watershed generally – may in turn have a serious effect on the breeding success of salmon, which are key to the entire ecosystem. However, in February 2008 a new round of agreements was signed, enforcing a system of "ecosystem-based management", which ambitiously aims to leave an intact environment behind after logging, while also delivering sustainable jobs and local prosperity.

Meanwhile, other threats loom on the horizon – if not already over it. The expansion of oil exploitation in the neighbouring landlocked province of Alberta, currently enjoying a "black gold rush", is already bringing the prospect of pipelines running to the British Columbia coast and of tanker traffic in waters that for more than three decades have enjoyed a tanker moratorium. Oil producers are also seeking to import liquefied natural gas, used in the extraction of bitumen on the oil fields (known as "oil sands" or "tar sands", excavated by large scale open-cast mining), from a terminal and pipeline to be established at the coastal town of Kitimat, in the heart of the Great Bear Rainforest. Elsewhere, there are proposals for numerous hydroelectric projects, as well as for the world's largest wind turbine farm, with related access roads and transmission lines likely to disrupt important wildlife habitats. The issue of logging may have been addressed, but the world has moved on, and with it new challenges are presenting themselves.

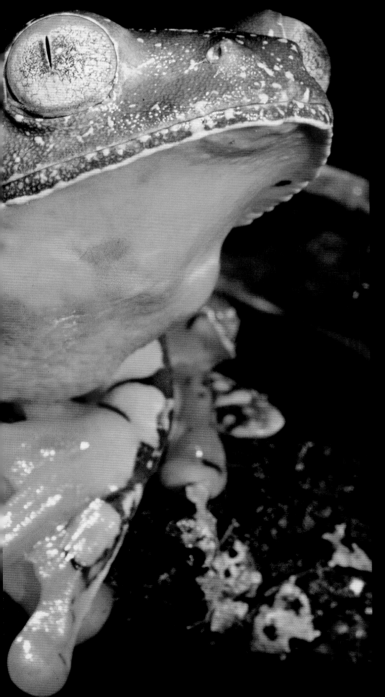

LATIN AMERICA

The rainforests of Central and South America are some of the most extensive and wildlife-rich of all. The Neotropics support a diverse range of rainforest habitats, from the dense mangroves of the Gulf of Mexico coastline through the mist-swathed cloudforests of the high cordillera then south to the temperate rainforests of the Chilean coast. However, one area stands out as truly remarkable: the mighty Amazon Basin, which supports the largest contiguous tract of lowland rainforest in the world. Defying all normal standards of biodiversity, Amazonia is an ecological reservoir on a scale that is difficult to comprehend. One-fifth of the world's oxygen is produced here, the home of forty per cent of the planet's surviving rainforest, one-third of all flowering plants and 20 per cent of the global supply of fresh water. With scientists making new discoveries on a daily basis, we have probably only scratched the surface in terms of what is really there.

LEFT Rainforest frogs include some of the most colourful and dramatic species found anywhere in the world. These are Fringed Leaf Frogs *Agalychnis craspedopus*, photographed in Amazonian Ecuador.

13. Into the Amazon: Ecuador's Yasuní National Park

The first Spanish adventurers to explore the Amazon rainforests, as part of their ill-fated search for El Dorado during the sixteenth century, faced a decidedly hostile environment. Much of what they encountered was unknown to them, but few of those new sights and sounds could have been as terrifying as the blood-curdling roars that echoed regularly through the treetops. With the Amazon rumoured to be the haunt of hideous man-eating monsters, those early explorers could have been forgiven for thinking that they were about to enter the portals of Hell itself. Today we know that what they described as the cries of banshees were actually the territorial calls of Red Howler Monkeys *Alouatta seniculus*, but in some respects parts of the mighty Amazon rainforest remain scarcely better understood today than 500 years ago.

Many early travellers attempted to penetrate the region via its rivers, among them the mighty River Napo. Ecuador's main Amazonian tributary runs for over 880 kilometres (550 miles) from headwaters on the slopes of some of the Andean chain's major volcanoes, including the famous Cotopaxi, down into the vastness of the Amazon Basin, where it joins the world's greatest river. During its journey the Napo is joined by numerous other smaller tributaries, so that it swells vastly during the rainy season and floods much of the forest immediately along its banks. For thousands of years the Napo has been of critical importance in the lives of the indigenous people who live nearby, and it continues to serve as an important communication artery for Ecuador generally.

On the southern side of the Napo, and in the heart of the Ecuadorian Amazon, lies Yasuní National Park, a wilderness area of mostly pristine rainforest covering some 688,000 hectares

OPPOSITE **The best way to travel in the Amazon rainforest is by boat, indeed in many areas this is the only feasible mode of transport. Traditional dugout canoes offer the chance to approach quietly, with local guides highly skilled at both steering the craft and spotting wildlife.**

RIGHT **Yasuní National Park is the ancestral home of various indigenous communities. These include the Huarani tribe, traditionally one the most hostile groups to outside influences. Here two men are preparing curare poison for blowpipes, which are still used for hunting.**

ABOVE The bizarre Hoatzin is a common sight along the waterways in Yasuní. Small groups gather in the bushes and trees, often with their wings drooped in characteristic pose. They fly clumsily and only for short distances.

(1.7 million acres) and designated a UNESCO Biosphere Reserve. The park is Ecuador's largest, and exceptionally diverse in terms of its plants and wildlife. A remarkable 473 different tree species and more than 100,000 insect species have been recorded in 1 hectare (2.5 acres) alone of forest here – quite possibly the highest density of anywhere in the world. The park is home to over 160 species of mammal, and is outstanding ornithologically, almost 600 different bird species having been recorded. With much of the forest still under-explored, the real total is likely to be even higher.

Yasuní is undoubtedly one of the best places to watch wildlife in the entire Amazon Basin and in recent years several facilities for ecotourism have been developed along the Napo River on the northern boundary of the park. Outstanding among these, and the only current option for staying inside the park proper, is the Napo Wildlife Centre Reserve. Both the reserve and its associated lodge were established – and are now managed – by the local Añangu community, many of whom work here as wildlife guides and in other tourism-related roles. The lodge is located on the shores of a small lake in the heart of the reserve, which covers 212 square kilometres (82 square miles) and contains a range of wildlife-rich habitats, from permanently dry rainforest *terra firme* through seasonally flooded forest *várzea* and permanently flooded forest *igapó*. The lodge is accessed only by traditional dugout canoe along the maze of waterways and oxbow lakes that lead to the lake from the Napo River itself. The journey to and fro offers superb wildlife viewing and is a fabulous introduction to the beauty and diversity of the Amazon. Huge iridescent blue *Morpho* butterflies look stunning in their lilting flight over the water along the channels, and the riverine vegetation and gallery forest are particularly productive for birds, and also for reptiles such as the Northern Caiman Lizard *Dracaena guianensis*, often seen stretched out along branches over the water. Canoe trips at dusk and after dark offer the chance to see bats and Black Caiman *Melanosuchus niger*, the latter often only detectable by the reflection of their eyes in torchlight, as well as the thrill of being paddled along a waterway lit either side by millions of fireflies.

Some 568 species of bird have been recorded on the reserve. These include five species of kingfisher, alongside typical Amazonian rainforest species such as jacamars, trogons and cotingas. One of the most obvious and interesting birds is the primitive-looking Hoatzin *Opisthocomus*

OPPOSITE There is a vast number of bat species in the Amazon, including many about which hardly anything is known. At night crowds of bats swoop low over the water feeding on insects, and during the day can be found roosting on tree trunks, rock faces and posts. These are Long-nosed Bats *Rhynchonycteris naso*.

hoatzin, usually seen loafing around in trees and shrubs next to the water. It is the only primarily leaf-eating (or folivorous) bird species, and has a specially adapted gut containing microflora which break down the otherwise indigestible leaf matter. Young Hoatzins are even more remarkable in that their wings have claws on the first and second digits, which enable the youngsters to clamber about the vegetation and even haul themselves out of the water on the rare occasions when they fall in.

A particular avian highlight at Napo takes place each morning at a series of clay licks near the river. Although parrots can also be seen from the reserve's impressive canopy tower, 36 metres (118 feet) high in a magnificent Kapok tree *Ceiba pentandra*, nothing compares with the sight of hundreds of these extraordinary birds noisily congregating on the areas of exposed soil. They are attracted by the minerals contained in the clay, which they eat to counteract the effect of the toxins present in some of the nuts and fruits on which they feed. Exactly how evolution effected such a remarkable connection is not clear, but as many as 10 different parrot species are known to visit the licks. The commoner among them – species such as Blue-headed Parrot *Pionus menstruus*, Cobalt-winged Parakeet *Brotogeris cyanoptera* and Dusky-headed Parakeet *Aratinga weddelli* – often gather in large associated flocks, although when they actually descend to eat the clay they tend to collect in smaller groups with those of their own species.

The first birds arrive shortly after dawn, flying in from their overnight roosts and at first perching warily in trees and shrubs near the lick before a few brave individuals finally take the plunge and drop down onto the clay itself. They are soon followed by the less courageous masses, and within seconds a raucous and spectacular show is in progress. Species such as Mealy Amazon *Amazona farinosa* and Black-headed Parrot *Pionites melanocephalus* often join the fray, and rarer visitors such as Scarlet Macaw *Ara macao* and Scarlet-shouldered Parrotlet *Touit huetii* occasionally turn up. Watching these colourful and engaging birds all jostling noisily side by side on the exposed slopes is one of the great attractions of Napo.

OPPOSITE The Napo clay licks are an outstanding location for watching parrots. Blinds have been constructed at two of the licks, enabling visitors to observe the large numbers of birds without disturbing them. In this shot are Mealy Amazons (the biggest birds), Blue-headed Parrots and Dusky-headed Parakeets (the latter mostly clinging to the cliff face).

RIGHT More than a dozen species of manakin have been recorded in Yasuní. They include the Wire-tailed Manakin *Pipra filicauda*, which exhibits both the colourful plumage and elaborate courtship display typical of this family.

LEFT Golden-mantle Tamarins move quickly through the undergrowth and canopy in search of food, and are hard to see well. This is a rather localized species, and appears to be restricted to eastern Ecuador and adjacent parts of Peru.

BELOW The eerie roars of Red Howler Monkeys are very much part of the lowland rainforest scene in Central and South America. They have relatively small home ranges and are highly sedentary, moving only short distances from day to day.

Although certain mammals sometimes visit the clay licks, including dramatic species such as Giant Anteater *Myrmecophaga tridactyla*, the most noticeable mammals to be seen on the reserve are usually primates. Eleven species are present here, of which six or seven are commonly recorded. Few visitors fail to see, or at least hear, Red Howler Monkeys. Howlers live in family clans of up to up to 35 individuals, although between eight and 15 is more usual, and their characteristic roaring is usually delivered from the high canopy at dawn and dusk, and sometimes just before or after rain. Essentially a series of accelerating and prolonged grunts delivered by the males, it can carry for up to 2 kilometres (slightly over 1 mile) in calm conditions. Females will sometimes join in with higher-pitched calls until several individuals can be chorusing simultaneously – a show-stopping performance by any standards.

The other species of primate resident at Napo are generally more discreet. Although highly localized, the attractive Golden-mantle Tamarin *Saguinus tripartitus* is quite common in certain favoured areas and can be observed in groups of between four and 10, leaping about the vegetation in search of fruit and insects. Dusky Titi Monkeys *Callicebus molloch* are also regularly seen, as are Common Squirrel Monkeys *Saimiri sciureus*. One of the area's most charismatic mammals, the Giant Otter *Pteronura brasiliensis*, has declined over much of its range in recent decades owing to hunting and habitat loss, but it remains relatively common here and visitors to Napo may even be lucky enough to see a pair or family party on the approach to the lodge. Attention is often first drawn by the otters' characteristic calls, sometimes delivered from the security of riverside vegetation; although shy, they are curious animals and will sometimes approach boats to get a better view of the occupants.

To date, the lack of easy access to Yasuní National Park has helped protect both the rainforest and its wildlife. However, areas of primary forest to the west and north-west have already been adversely affected by logging and road construction, and the potential exploitation of the extensive reserves of oil on which the park itself sits – estimated at 1 billion barrels' worth – is a continuing source of concern for conservationists and of potential conflict with indigenous communities. Drilling for oil is already a fact of life in parts of eastern Ecuador, with large tracts of rainforest destroyed or scarred by networks of roads, drilling rigs, processing plants and pollution. The spectre now looms of a similar catastrophe taking place actually inside the park boundaries, on the grounds that the financial rewards from oil will hugely benefit a low-income country like Ecuador. At the time of writing, the Ecuadorian government was engaging in a debate with the international community about the idea of being compensated financially by the developed world for *not* drilling in the park, thereby saving it. If successful, these negotiations could have important implications for the future of protected areas elsewhere in the developing world.

LEFT **Poison dart frogs** (this is *Dendrobates duellmani*) are widespread in Amazonia. The toxic excretions they produce are traditionally smeared by indigenous peoples on their arrows and blowdarts for use in hunting. The frogs' bright colours serve as a warning to predators that they do not make good eating.

OPPOSITE **Tarantulas** are common and widespread in the rainforest, but not always easy to see. They spend much of the day in crevices and burrows, often located in and around large buttress roots, emerging only under cover of darkness to go hunting.

RIGHT **Without the advantage** of toxins, other frog species use different techniques to deter predators. This Broad-headed Tree Frog *Phrynohyaas resinifictrix* is inflating its air sacs defensively, thereby appearing larger than it really is.

14. New Discoveries in the Cloudforest of Tapichalaca, Ecuador

In 1997 a group of ornithologists exploring an area of remote cloudforest in southern Ecuador caught a glimpse of a bird totally new to science. Although known to local people by its explosive and characteristic call, this species had probably never actually been seen by anyone before, owing to its furtive habits and the difficult nature of its habitat – dense bamboo thickets on the steep and thickly forested mountain of Cerro Tapichalaca on the eastern slopes of the Andes. Whereas many recent avian discoveries have involved variations of the proverbial LBJ – "Little Brown Job", the new bird was definitely not in that category. It proved to be a previously undescribed species of large antpitta, standing 23 centimetres (9 inches) high and boldly marked, with a black and white face, olive-rufous back and wings and grey underparts. Particularly striking are its bright blue legs, on which it runs and scrambles through the virtually impenetrable undergrowth typical of the Andean cloudforest. This remarkably striking bird was given the name of Jocotoco Antpitta *Grallaria ridgelyi*; "Jocotoco" after the local description of its distinctive and unusual call, and *ridgelyi*, after Robert Ridgely, one of the foremost authorities on the avifauna of Latin America and the first biologist actually to see one.

This extraordinary discovery was effectively the starting pistol in a race against time. Selective logging and the clearing of forest for cattle pasture had already taken place at Tapichalaca, with many of the mature trees removed, and the whole forest was at risk of clearance and burning. With almost the entire world population of the new antpitta confined to this relatively small area, the virtual extinction of the species within months of its scientific discovery looked possible unless something was done. Even now, a decade later, field research in neighbouring mountains has found only a further 10 or so pairs in addition to the approximately 15 pairs present in the original area.

OPPOSITE **Mist and low cloud are almost constantly present at Tapichalaca. The high humidity levels and moisture help ensure optimal conditions for the profusion of epiphytes that grow both at ground level and on the larger trees and shrubs.**

RIGHT **One of the rarest birds in the world, the Jocotoco Antpitta is restricted to a small area of cloudforest in remote southern Ecuador. Concerted conservation action is in hand to secure its future.**

FAR RIGHT **The antpittas live in very dense undergrowth, composed largely of mossy bamboo. The demanding terrain makes study of this elusive bird particularly difficult, and much remains to be discovered about its ecology and requirements.**

BELOW The rediscovery of *Bomarea longipes* at Tapichalaca, more than a century after the type specimen was collected and taken to England, was one of the great botanic events in Ecuador in recent decades. Detective work such as this continues to engage scientists in rainforests across the globe.

RIGHT Mammals at Tapichalaca include White-fronted Capuchin *Cebus albifrons*, which although primarily a lowland species does occur up to altitudes of 2,000 metres (6,500 feet) or so. Individuals can be highly variable in fur colour, ranging from almost white to mid-brown.

An Ecuadorian conservation organization, the Fundación Jocotoco, was created to establish both a reserve in the area and the means by which both the bird and its habitat could be safeguarded. Within a year of the Jocotoco Antpitta being discovered, the Fundación had purchased several parcels of land in the forest and work has continued since then to build up a reserve now covering 3,750 hectares (9,300 acres) ranging from 1,700 to 3,500 metres (5,500–11,500 feet) in altitude. Although primarily composed of temperate cloudforest, Tapichalaca Reserve also includes areas of subtropical rainforest at lower levels. At about 2,900 metres (9,500 feet) the cloudforest gives way to elfin woodland, a dense community of diminutive stunted trees and shrubs, reaching only 1 metre (3 feet) or so in height and covered in lichens, algae and bryophytes. Even such modest trees cannot grow at altitudes higher than 3,300 metres (10,800 feet) or so, above which *paramó* – a type of grassland with low shrubs – dominates. This cold and windy landscape supports montane flora such as gentians, as well as some of the reserve's most interesting mammals (see below).

Cloudforest is the dominant ecosystem on the eastern slopes of the Andes between approximately 1,500 and 3,000 metres (4,900–9,900 feet). Moisture from the warmer lowland forests of the Amazon Basin below rises and cools, a process accentuated by the fall in ambient temperature as altitude increases. The result is very high levels of condensation and precipitation, with almost constant heavy mists, low cloud cover, drizzle and rain all typical of this environment. Mornings may dawn bright, but conditions usually soon deteriorate and several days may pass at a time without any sun at all. Not surprisingly, cloudforest vegetation is exceptionally lush and characterized by an abundance of ferns and tree ferns, mosses, lichens, bromeliads and epiphytes, especially orchids, as well as palms and flowering shrubs (the latter being especially important for hummingbirds). Tapichalaca is typical in this respect and is especially notable for its dense stands of mossy bamboo (*Chusquea* spp.), the specific habitat of the Jocotoco Antpitta.

The forest vegetation here can be virtually impenetrable and access is exceedingly difficult away from the trails that have been cut to give limited visitor access to the reserve. The ground is permanently wet, visibility often poor and the foliage almost constantly drenched in mist or rain. Annual rainfall levels are in the region of 5 metres (16.5 feet) and the reserve is characterized by very steep slopes and ridges, so conditions for human visitors are not among the easiest. Yet this is a magical place, and it would be an insensitive soul indeed who could resist its charm. What makes it such a rewarding place to explore is the sheer diversity and profusion of life, a spectacle made all the more exciting by the knowledge that this forest represents a real frontier in terms of

LEFT Owing to the virtually permanent cloud and mist, most visitors to Tapichalaca fail to have a good view of the high mountain ridge of Cerro Tapichalaca. Largely inaccessible, the densely vegetated slopes are home to many of the reserve's special plants, animals and birds.

our natural history knowledge. New species are being recorded all the time and doubtless many more await discovery.

Although the reserve at Tapichalaca was established primarily to protect the Jocotoco Antpitta, ongoing research is revealing that this is a very important site indeed for many other forms of flora and fauna. Cloudforest is typified by high levels of biodiversity and is particularly notable for the rate of endemism, which is greater than at lower altitudes. For example, in the tropical Andes some 40 per cent of bird species are endemic, compared to 19 per cent in Amazonia. The Jocotoco Antpitta aside, it is already clear that Tapichalaca is also outstanding botanically. Even in an orchid hotspot like Ecuador, where over 4,000 different species have already been recorded (the most of any country in the world), including some 1,500 endemics, the reserve is special. Despite its relatively small size, it supports between 150 and 200 of the endemics and is home to over 30 orchid species that have proved to be totally new to science and restricted to the reserve and its buffer zone. As research continues, so the discoveries increase. For example, long-lost species have been relocated on the reserve, among them the dramatic vine *Bomarea longipes*, hitherto known only from the type specimen held in the herbarium at the Royal Botanic Garden Kew following its collection in 1876 from an unknown site in Ecuador. Following a chance rediscovery, this has now been shown to have been Tapichalaca.

The reserve's amphibians are also causing a stir. An impressive new species of apparently endemic tree frog, *Hyloscirtus tapichalaca*, was described in 2003 and is still known only from the vegetation along a single stream. This extreme level of habitat specialization underlines not only the exceptional refinement of the ecological niches in the cloudforest environment but also the

LEFT TOP AND BOTTOM **Ongoing research is confirming Tapichalaca to be a very important site for amphibians. The extremely localized and endemic *Hyloscirtus tapichalaca* (top) is one of the more remarkable, but also recorded from the reserve is *Eleutherodactylus galdi* (bottom), regarded as "near threatened" globally.**

LEFT TOP AND BOTTOM **Several** species of dramatic hummingbird are attracted to the feeders erected next to the lodge at Tapichalaca. Among them are the Long-tailed Sylph *Aglaiocercus kingi* (top) and the Amethyst-throated Sunangel *Heliangelus amethysticollis* (bottom).

vulnerability of the species that have evolved to occupy such refined niches. A small change in their environment could bring about their extinction, as occurred most dramatically with the Golden Toad *Bufo periglenes* in one of the world's other great cloudforests, Monteverde in Costa Rica.

Undoubtedly the most impressive mammal present on the reserve at Tapichalaca – although actual sightings are very infrequent – is the Spectacled Bear *Tremarctos ornatus*. South America's only true bear, this enigmatic species is widely but thinly distributed along the Andean chain from western Venezuela south to Peru and Bolivia. It inhabits a wide range of habitats but is essentially montane-dwelling and at Tapichalaca is most often seen in the elfin woodland or out on the *paramó*. Globally, its numbers have fallen sharply in recent decades as a result of hunting and habitat destruction. However, Tapichalaca and the neighbouring Podocarpus National Park remain a stronghold for the species and there are signs that conservation measures are now working and that the Ecuadorian population at least may be stabilizing. Although omnivorous, Spectacled Bears are mainly vegetarian and especially partial to fruit, *Puya* plants, bamboo and bromeliads. Signs of their presence include discarded fragments of bromeliads, torn apart by the bears to reach the hearts, which are a particular favourite. The other large mammal occurring at Tapichalaca is the Mountain Tapir *Tapirus pinchaque*. This species is restricted to Colombia, Ecuador and extreme north-western Peru, and although quite common on the reserve, is shy and rarely seen. The most usual sign of its presence is a crashing sound as it rushes off through the undergrowth.

The purchase of the forest at Tapichalaca to save the Jocotoco Antpitta marked only the beginning for the Fundación Jocotoco, which now owns and manages eight reserves across Ecuador. Each was chosen because it is home to rare or threatened species of birds otherwise not protected within Ecuador's network of national parks, but as at Tapichalaca research has revealed every reserve to have much more than a purely ornithological claim to justify its acquisition. With a vast range of different microclimates and habitats, Ecuador is one of the most biologically diverse countries on the planet, but, as elsewhere in South America, it has suffered extensive deforestation. Only 20–25 per cent of its original tree cover survives, often in poor condition and increasingly fragmented. Population pressure across much of the country is continuing to intensify, and the constant demand for farmland is an ongoing threat to the surviving forests. With much of Ecuador's flora and fauna highly localized, many species are vulnerable to extinction if forests continue to be cleared. However, as scientific research establishes greater understanding of which species are present where, and why, it should become possible to develop conservation strategies that can help protect the greatest number of species within the land and financial resources that are available. For example, a few carefully located reserves in 'centres of endemism' can provide protection to a high proportion of the most threatened species.

Meanwhile, conservation work at Tapichalaca is primarily concerned with improving the Jocotoco Antpitta's habitat and with the reforestation of some sizeable tracts of forest which, before acquisition by the Fundación, had been cleared and converted to pasture for grazing cattle. Natural regeneration and careful replanting are improving the cloudforest cover and connecting areas of forest that had become fragmented. This increase in available habitat is helping secure the future of this remarkable reserve and its wildlife, and should also reduce Tapichalaca's vulnerability to the adverse effects of anticipated global warming.

RIGHT **Flowering shrubs such as this *Tibouchina* sp. attract a variety of insects and hummingbirds. Both serve as important pollinating agents in the cloudforest environment.**

Original extent of Atlantic Rainforest in Brazil

BRAZIL

Recife
Murici Biological Reserve
Salvador

ATLANTIC OCEAN

Itatiaia National Park
São Paulo
Serra dos Órgãos National Park
Rio de Janeiro
Poço das Antas Biological Reserve
Superagüi National Park
Florianópolis

N

15. The Last Remnants of Brazil's Atlantic Rainforests

Once running for some 2,400 kilometres (1,490 miles) along almost the entire eastern seaboard of Brazil, the Atlantic rainforests or *Mata Atlântica* have now been reduced to only 6–7 per cent of their former extent. What was once a virtually unbroken belt cloaking the upland ranges and coastal lowlands is now reduced to a handful of widely scattered fragments. This scale of destruction is probably unmatched anywhere else in the world, the fate of these forests rendered all the more tragic by the fact that in terms of flora and fauna they are one of the richest habitats of all.

The Atlantic forests are one of the hottest of biodiversity hotspots. They support some 20,000 species of vascular plant, for example, with 8,000 or so of those endemic. Up to 50 per cent of the trees growing here are found nowhere else, and can occur at a bewildering density: as many as 476 species have been recorded within a single hectare (2.5 acres), more than in an equivalent section of typical Amazonian rainforest. Seventy of the 260 mammal species found in the Atlantic forests are endemic, and include several critically endangered

LEFT The Serra dos Órgãos National Park is an excellent site for birds, with the large species total including some of the highly localized Atlantic forest endemics. Established in 1939, the park covers 110 square kilometres (42.5 square miles) and is only one hour's drive from Rio city.

OPPOSITE The appealing looks of the Golden Lion Tamarin have partly contributed to its current low population levels. Highly prized in the pet trade, many hundreds were trapped and exported before the practice was made illegal in the 1970s.

LEFT The Atlantic Forest ecoregion has one of the world's largest totals of recorded butterflies. Butterflies and moths are important indicators of environmental "well-being", being among the first groups to decline when conditions deteriorate even slightly. This is an Orsis Bluewing *Myscelia orsis*.

primates. The region's birdlife is equally exclusive, with around 200 endemic species, some of which are restricted to just one small area of remaining forest and are therefore highly vulnerable to extinction. Meanwhile, scientists are still only scratching the surface of the invertebrate populations; but with over 2,000 species of butterfly already identified, all the signs are that other insect groups will be equally prolific.

Separated from the rainforests of the Amazon by the *cerrado*, a huge expanse of savanna and dry forest, the Atlantic forests evolved largely in isolation, which helps explain the high levels of endemism found here. The forest ecoregion contains a mix of vegetation types, from tracts of mangroves around the river estuaries through evergreen lowland forest on the coastal plain and then rising to montane rainforest and elfin woodland at higher altitudes. The rainforest habitats are restricted to the coastal lowlands and eastward-facing mountain slopes; on the other side of the upland ranges the evergreen forests are largely replaced by deciduous vegetation. However, there are areas of coastal deciduous woodland, known as *restinga*, found on particularly sandy and nutrient-poor soils. All the region's forests have been seriously reduced in extent and quality by human activity.

Whereas in most of the world's rainforests the process of wholesale destruction is less than 100 years old, in this part of Brazil man has been clearing the forest for centuries. The first European colonists settled the coastal lowlands in the sixteenth century, and immediately set about removing the tree cover. This was largely to make way for agricultural land, particularly cattle pasture, and – in the north-east of the region – sugar cane plantations, but the timber itself was in much demand for construction and as firewood. The wood from some species of tree was particularly prized, notably Brazilian Rosewood *Dalbergia nigra* and Pau Brasil *Caesalpina echinata*, popular for a wide range of uses that extended to the making of furniture and musical instruments. Also known as Pernambuco, Pau Brasil even gave its name to the newly "discovered" country, the colour of its wood described as *brassa* (a reference to its rich, burning-red hue), the term from which the name Brazil was subsequently derived. Both varieties of tree were subject to uncontrolled logging and by the 1600s were already becoming rare.

As the human population increased, so demand for timber, firewood and charcoal grew, the native forests subsequently replaced in part by expanses of monoculture eucalyptus. The development of urban centres and their associated infrastructure took a further toll on the already depleted forests, with agricultural expansion, economic development and uncontrolled mining activity all hastening the rate of destruction. Today the Atlantic coast region is Brazil's industrial powerhouse, and with the 70 per cent or so of the Brazilian population living in the Atlantic littoral in megacities such as São Paulo and Rio de Janeiro, pressure on the forest remains intense. Many of the surviving pockets of forest are directly on the urban fringe, under continued pressure from landless squatters seeking to establish smallholdings and, along the coastal strip, from tourism-related development.

As soon as they are fragmented by roads or other aspects of disruptive human activity, areas of forest easily deteriorate in quality. The so-called "edge effect" has a serious impact; the edges of tropical forest are usually drier, hotter and more exposed to wind and violent rainfall than the more sheltered areas within, and so in small forest fragments species dependent on "deep forest" conditions soon die out as the conditions of the edges start to dictate the environment throughout the forest fragment.

In recent decades most of the conservation attention in the Atlantic forests has been focused on the endemic primates and birds. The region's monkeys include the largest South American members of the family, the Northern and Southern Muriquis *Brachyteles hypoxanthus* and *B. arachnoides*,

BELOW Bromeliads are abundant in the Atlantic rainforests, growing wherever they find a suitable niche. This can be down on the ground, high in the tree canopy or anywhere in between. Bromeliads store water in their cup-like interiors, reservoirs that in turn are home to a wealth of invertebrates.

two closely related species of spider monkey found only in sections of the *Mata Atlântica*, and all four species of lion tamarin, which are among the smallest of primates and found only here. All are threatened with extinction. They first came to outside attention in 1519, when the chronicler Antonio Pigafetta, travelling with explorer Fernando Magellan, described "beautiful, simian-like cats similar to small lions". These were probably Golden Lion Tamarins *Leontopithecus rosalia*, one of the most beautiful of all primates and one that for centuries has suffered from habitat destruction and an enduring popularity in the pet trade. By the time this trade was banned in the 1970s, it had become clear that the species was on the very brink of disappearing for good.

Today the Golden Lion is found in a handful of relict populations, notably at the 6,500-hectare (16,000-acre) Poço das Antas reserve. A successful captive breeding programme has made possible the introduction of zoo-bred animals to the wild, and such releases now account for 40 per cent or so of wild animals. With a total world population now in excess of 1,500 (up from 200 in the early 1970s), the future is looking brighter for the Golden Lion. However, further expansion into areas from which tamarins have been extirpated will be difficult to secure without improved habitat protection and management. The species therefore remains on red alert.

The three other species of lion tamarin are equally endangered. The Golden-headed Lion Tamarin *L. chrysomelas* has the largest population, with a few thousand still holding out in forest fragments in Bahia state, but their habitat continues to dwindle. Around 1,000 Black Lion Tamarins *L. chrysopygus* survive in São Paulo state. But the situation of the Black-faced Lion Tamarin *L. caissara*, only described to science in 1990, is more critical, with possibly as few as 300 left at a handful of locations in the states of São Paulo and Paraná, the majority on the island of Superagüi. Concerted conservation efforts are now in hand to try to secure the future of these species. Lion tamarins appear to have always been restricted to lowland forests, and so

LEFT AND RIGHT **Two classic endemic birds of the Atlantic rainforest: the Saffron Toucanet *Pteroglossus bailloni* (left) and the Blue or Swallow-tailed Manakin *Chiroxiphia caudata* (right). Such species have become increasingly scarce and localized as their habitat has been destroyed, with some also suffering from the illegal bird trade.**

were immediately vulnerable when these began to be cleared in the 1500s. Their populations have consequently been in decline for centuries, and the reduced genetic viability of small groups surviving in isolated vestiges of forest is one impediment to future population growth.

The habitat destruction that has had such an impact on the lion tamarins has equally affected the region's birdlife. As many as a quarter of the Atlantic forest avian endemics are considered threatened with extinction, a situation made more acute by the fact that some of them occur in only the tiniest fragments of habitat. For example, the 30-square-kilometre (11.5-square-mile) Murici Biological Reserve in the state of Alagoas is home to 13 species under threat, two of which are yet to be recorded anywhere else but in this section of forest. Despite ostensibly being a protected area, forest cover here has shrunk considerably over the last 30 years as a result of illegal logging and of fires that spread from nearby sugar cane plantations.

Two of the most important areas for montane forest birds are in Rio state, the Serra dos Órgãos National Park and the Itatiaia National Park. The latter's Três Picos trail is one of *the* birding spots in South America, and leads through thick forest, including dense tracts of bamboo. Many species of antbird, antpitta, antshrike and antthrush occur here, alongside a bewildering variety of tanagers and other flagship forest species such as toucans and cotingas. Although lengthy hikes can be required to see some of the scarcer and more elusive species, many of the commoner – but no less stunning – birds are readily drawn to the feeders set up specially for them in the gardens of local guesthouses and hotels.

Despite the loss of so much of the Atlantic rainforests, there are signs of a more encouraging future. Brazilian conservationists are increasingly mobilized and influential, and the recent growth in ecotourism, and particularly birding holidays aimed at overseas visitors, is generating income for local communities that have traditionally exploited the forest to beyond the point of sustainability. Habitat restoration programmes aimed at creating corridors between forest fragments (with local

LEFT **The Black Jacobin** *Florisuga fusca* **is a type of hummingbird restricted to the eastern parts of Brazil and some adjacent areas of Argentina, Paraguay and Uruguay. It is a common visitor to feeders erected in Itatiaia National Park.**

RIGHT Some 300 species of reptile have been recorded in the Atlantic forests, roughly one-third of which are endemic. Snakes are well represented here, especially the *Bothrops* genus. This is a Two-striped Forest-pitviper *Bothrops bilineata*.

ABOVE AND LEFT **Fragmented across their entire historical range, the Atlantic rainforests now comprise a widely scattered series of wooded "islands". Some of these are very small, surrounded by plantation monoculture such as coffee (above) or by open pasture (left). Restoring connectivity between forest remnants is a major conservation priority.**

BELOW The Seven-coloured Tanager *Tangara fastuosa* is known from fewer than 20 sites towards the north-eastern end of the Atlantic rainforest belt. This species appears to nest mainly in large bromeliads and so is dependent on mature rainforest with plenty of epiphytes.

farmers growing tree seedlings for reafforestation schemes), and the captive breeding of vulnerable species, both hold out hope that it may prove possible to reclaim some of the ground lost over the past five centuries. Paradoxically, the proximity of some surviving fragments to large urban conurbations could become a strength, as such green areas are valued as "urban lungs".

Huge problems remain, however. Only one-third or so of the surviving *Mata Atlântica* is officially protected, and there is often little effective enforcement on the ground. Some of the most productive wildlife areas are privately owned and well-managed *fazendas* (farms and estates), but there are plenty of less wildlife-friendly private landowners, and on government- and state-owned land, wildlife and habitats continue to be equally vulnerable. In areas – often the more remote sites, in the north of the region – where ownership is unclear, or not regularly policed, small-scale clearance and illegal hunting continue to be major problems. Yet perhaps a corner has been turned. In recent years bird species thought extinct have been rediscovered, and even species previously unknown to science have come to light. Even when reduced to such a tiny vestige of its former self, the Atlantic rainforest continues to spring surprises.

16. The Jaguars of Iwokrama, Guyana

The Amazon Basin contains the greatest expanse of tropical rainforest in the world, at least four times larger than either of the next two largest such forests, in Congo and Indonesia. Some 85 per cent of South America's rainforest is found here, yet some of the most unspoilt and wildlife-rich forests are located outside the Basin proper, on one of two ancient upland areas known as "shields". Once part of the same vast landscape feature, the Guiana and Brazilian shields were divorced from each other by the formation of the Amazon River and its associated floodplain some 12 million years ago. These shields predate the formation of the Andes, and so are responsible for most of the sediments in the central and eastern Amazon Basin. Today the Guiana Shield supports the largest single tract of pristine tropical rainforest in the world.

From the shield's northern edge, lowland rainforest continues virtually uninterrupted for hundreds of kilometres to reach the shores of the Caribbean. Low human population density has helped ensure its survival. The country of Guyana, for example, covers 215,000 square kilometres (83,000 square miles) but is home to only 750,000 people, most of them concentrated along the coast. The interior is very sparsely populated and remains largely covered in dense rainforest, much of it only lightly explored by scientists. The sheer scale of the forest is all too apparent as soon as one leaves the capital, Georgetown, by air. Tropical vegetation extends as far as the eye can see, a vast blanket of dark green, broken periodically by areas of open savannah.

LEFT **Much of Guyana is still covered by primary lowland rainforest. Located at the heart of the country, the Iwokrama reserve was gifted by the Guyanan government to the Commonwealth in 1989 as a focus for pioneering conservation projects.**

OPPOSITE **Jaguars exude power and grace. Once found as far north as the southern United States and well south into Argentina, the species has contracted in range and declined in numbers as a result of hunting and habitat destruction.**

LEFT The world's largest water lily, *Victoria amazonica*, with a juvenile Black Caiman *Caiman niger*. Although caimans are common at Iwokrama, they are under pressure elsewhere in South America due to overhunting for their skin.

BELOW Rainforest snakes in Guyana include the Emerald Tree Boa *Corallus caninus*, a highly arboreal species which is hardly, if ever, seen on the ground. Mature specimens can reach lengths of up to 2 metres (6.5 feet).

With so much of its forest intact and supporting a wealth of wildlife that is under increasing pressure elsewhere, Guyana has vast potential as a destination for ecotourism and as a showcase for the sustainable use of the forest and its products. This complex and sensitive process is already under way at the Iwokrama International Centre for Rainforest Conservation and Development. Conceived as an innovative flagship project, a "living laboratory" for scientific research, ecotourism and sustainable forestry, the centre is responsible for the management of the vast reserve of Iwokrama Forest, an arrangement that is probably unique in protected area conservation. Significantly, the legislation establishing the reserve recognized indigenous rights, and local communities play a role in the day-to-day running of the Centre and reserve.

Declared by the Guyanan government in 1989, the reserve covers 3,700 square kilometres (1,450 square miles) of pristine lowland rainforest in central Guyana, bisected by the road that leads from Georgetown into Brazil. Up to 12 different forest types have been distinguished within Iwokrama, but broadly speaking the northern 75 per cent of the reserve can be classified as tropical moist forest and the southern 25 per cent as tropical dry forest. No particular tree species dominates, with Soft Wallaba *Eperua falcata*, Baromalli *Catostemma* spp., Black Kakeralli *Eschweilera subglandosa*, Wamara *Swartzia leiocalycina*, Mora *Mora excelsa*, Crabwood *Carapa guianensis* and Greenheart *Chlorocardium rodiei* all common. Some of these species have high commercial value; Crabwood is used to make furniture, for example, and the oil from its seeds has a wide range of applications, from insect repellent and homeopathic remedies to soap and candles. Greenheart, which is restricted to the Guiana Shield, is especially valued for its durability in salt water and is used worldwide in the construction of bridges and docks. The presence of such a variety of commercially significant species makes Iwokrama an ideal location for the development of sustainable tropical forestry.

Home to at least 1,500 species of flora, 200 of mammal, 500 of birds, 420 of fish, and 150 of amphibians and reptiles, Iwokrama is the best understood ecosystem on the Guiana Shield. Yet new discoveries are being made all the time, and the real levels of biodiversity are only now becoming clear. Many species of forest-dwelling mammal are certainly more common here than almost anywhere else in their range. In particular, the reserve is developing a reputation as being one of the best places in the world to see Jaguar *Panthera onca*. This shy and elusive cat is widely distributed across much of Central and northern South America but is under intense pressure over most of its range. Illegal hunting, habitat destruction and disturbance have reduced its

numbers to a dangerously low ebb in many regions, with numerous cases of local extinction and signs of a general population reduction in most of the countries in which it is resident. Its current distribution is approximately 50 per cent smaller than was the case in the early 1900s.

Although the Jaguar most immediately resembles the Leopard *Panthera pardus* in general appearance, in terms of ecology and behaviour it can more usefully be regarded as a New World equivalent of the Tiger *Panthera tigris*. Immensely powerful, Jaguars are probably the strongest of all the big cats, kilo for kilo. Stocky, muscular and broad-headed, they have a distinctive profile and rely on stealth to stalk their prey, usually pouncing at close range and killing by a single bite to the head. Over 80 different species have been recorded as menu items for Jaguars, ranging from large domestic livestock (a continuing source of conflict with humans in some parts of their range) down to birds, fish and amphibians. At Iwokrama the most common prey species are Capybara *Hydrochaeris hydrochaeris*, peccaries and deer.

Jaguars are as catholic in their choice of habitat as in prey. While they can occur in surprisingly open country, including grassland and even semi-desert in parts of their range, they generally prefer more thickly vegetated terrain with tracts of undergrowth in which to hunt. They are perhaps most typically found in the rainforest environment, and particularly near water. They are excellent swimmers and at Iwokrama have even been seen crossing the mighty Essequibo River on the reserve's eastern side, no mean feat for a cat, however powerful. Although Jaguars are mostly nocturnal, and so dawn and dusk are the most likely times to glimpse one, at Iwokrama sightings are not uncommon during the middle of the day. As ever, it is a question of luck, but one of the best places to look out for them is in the forest edge along the roadside, where tracks are a regular sight, as indeed they are in the mud along water courses.

Large male Jaguars can tip the scales at over 130 kilograms (290 pounds), but these tend to be those living in more open country. Forest-dwelling animals are lighter in weight, usually no heavier than 90 kilograms (200 pounds), which may reflect the generally smaller size of the prey available to them in this environment. And whilst all Jaguars have the characteristically patterned coat, the actual coloration is highly variable. The base colour ranges from reddish brown to yellow, and the pattern and size of the markings differ greatly between individuals. Evidence seems to suggest that Jaguars living in rainforest are generally darker than those in

FAR LEFT The Jaguar's distinctive coat helps provide highly effective camouflage in the dappled forest environment. The best chance of a good view is when an animal emerges into a clearing or onto a track, or when one is encountered wading or swimming across a river.

LEFT Iwokrama's canopy walkway gives superb views into the mid- and upper tree canopy. Early morning is an excellent time for birding here, with a range of otherwise secretive species at their most active and visible before the heat of the day sets in.

open areas such as the Pantanal (another stronghold for the species) – again probably an evolutionary response to the different prevailing conditions. As with the Leopard, there is also a rare melanistic form of Jaguar, probably accounting for no more than six per cent of all animals.

The most conspicuous mammals at Iwokrama are usually primates. One of the best places to try and see them is in the forest around the canopy walkway, 154 metres (505 feet) long and constructed of suspension bridges and canopy observation decks. Thirty metres (100 feet) high, it gives superb views into the canopy. The most immediately obvious primates are usually Red Howler Monkeys *Alouatta seniculus*, often heard "roaring" from the canopy in the early morning and evening. Also common, but rather more unobtrusive as they sit quietly feeding on fruit and seeds, are Guianan Saki Monkeys *Pithecia pithecia*, best identified by their shaggy coat and exceptionally bushy tail. The males also have a distinctive white face. The largest primate in the reserve is the Black Spider Monkey *Ateles paniscus*, often seen or heard crashing noisily through the canopy in search of fruit and flowers. When reaching for food it will often dangle precariously from branches, secured by its extraordinary prehensile tail. This species has a decidedly ape-like appearance and is often intolerant of humans; particularly irritable individuals have been recorded stamping their feet, shaking vegetation and even breaking off branches and throwing them at human "intruders" down below.

Birdlife is outstanding in the reserve and features many of the classic Neotropical rainforest species. Two especially notable species are the magnificent Harpy Eagle *Harpia harpyja*, South America's largest raptor but now rare over much of its range, and the remarkable Guianan Cock-of-the-rock *Rupicola rupicola*. A member of the cotinga family, this species has one of the world's most elaborate avian courtship rituals. The brightly coloured males – a stunning combination of orange and black, with a thick fan of feathers from the base of the bill to the back of the neck – gather in communal "leks", discrete areas in the rainforest understorey. Each male clears a patch of ground and will then start displaying, striking various poses and postures. These are designed to impress female birds, which gather nearby and watch the show before choosing to mate with a particularly impressive individual. A male's "ace card" is his fan, which he will excitedly show off side-on, to maximum advantage. Often several males will display competitively within a few metres of each other, surely one of the great rainforest sights.

OPPOSITE **Male cock-of-the-rocks are unmistakable and especially dramatic when displaying at their leks. These are often located near rocky outcrops, which loom up out of the forest floor and in which the females build their nests.**

ABOVE **Black Spider Monkeys often live in quite large troops, with several males accompanied y roughly twice as many females and various youngsters. Like all monkeys, this species uses a wide variety of visual communication methods, with facial gestures particularly important.**

17. The Rainforest Birds
of the West Indies

When Christopher Columbus sailed into the Caribbean on his first two voyages of discovery in 1492 and 1493, the islands he encountered were largely covered in luxuriant rainforest. This was an environment in which the indigenous human population lived for the most part harmoniously and sustainably, the forest providing almost all of their needs. Yet the European settlement that followed in Columbus's wake was to change this picture dramatically. The felling and export of lucrative hardwoods such as mahogany were already well in hand by the end of the sixteenth century, and subsequent centuries saw the rapid clearance of native forest to make way for plantation crops such as sugar cane, cotton, tobacco and bananas. The enforced slavery of the native Amerindians, and subsequently imported slave labour from Africa, made this process possible.

Today most Caribbean islands have little left of their original vegetation, their appearance now markedly different from the heavily wooded landscapes described by early European colonizers. Antigua and Barbados, for example, have lost 95 per cent of their native forest, and on only a few islands do meaningful tracts of rainforest survive. These are usually confined to relatively inaccessible locations on steep mountainsides, the rugged nature of the slopes having saved their trees from the axe, chainsaw and tractor. Lowland rainforest is a rare survival indeed in the Caribbean, and even at higher altitudes the forest is often fragmented and degraded by the presence of introduced plantation tree species.

OPPOSITE **The St Lucia Parrot has been saved from extinction in the wild, but further expansion of its numbers remains problematic due to lack of habitat. Conservation programmes aimed at improving degraded areas of forest will certainly help.**

BELOW **As elsewhere in the Caribbean, the surviving tracts of rainforest on St Lucia are mostly to be found where the terrain is relatively inaccessible. Forest still cloaks the steep slopes of The Pitons, twin volcanic peaks overlooking Soufrière Bay.**

ABOVE Once extensively hunted for its supposedly tasty flesh, the Mountain Chicken is now under severe pressure. Disease and habitat loss have combined to make the future of this fascinating creature look increasingly uncertain.

However, the island of Dominica has retained 60 per cent or so of original rainforest and is now one of the top ecological destinations in the West Indies. In particular, the Northern Forest Reserve holds some of the most pristine rainforest in the whole Caribbean region, and the Syndicate section of the reserve is the best place to look for Dominica's most distinguished bird: the Imperial Amazon or Sisserou *Amazona imperialis*. Endemic to the island and its undoubted avian highlight, the Imperial is the largest of the amazons (reaching a length of up to 48 centimetres/19 inches) and one of the rarest parrots in the world, with a total population of fewer than 200 individuals. These are confined to areas of pristine and undisturbed rainforest over rugged terrain, particularly favouring sheltered valleys and living mostly at altitudes of 600–1,300 metres (1,950–4,300 feet), although they will come lower to forage when food supplies are limited higher up.

They are not easy birds to see, being generally retiring and rather quiet by parrot standards, a distinct contrast with the much more gregarious and noisy Red-necked Amazon or Jacquot *Amazona arausiaca*, also endemic to Dominica and with which Imperials will sometimes associate. More often, they are found either singly or in pairs, almost always keeping to the high canopy where they move rather sedately through the foliage, feeding on fruits. Once a widespread and common bird, the population of Imperials was steadily reduced by habitat loss, by hunting for food and by trapping for the pet trade. By the early 1990s there may have been fewer than 100 birds remaining in the wild and, although numbers have since increased, the bird's low reproductive rate – pairs breed only every other year and raise only one chick – is hampering further recovery.

In addition to Northern Forest Reserve, the Imperial Amazon can be found in Morne Diablotin National Park and the Central Forest Reserve, as well as in the southern section of the dramatically beautiful Morne Trois Pitons National Park. Declared a World Heritage Site in 1997, this park is famous for its volcanic crater lakes and spectacular waterfalls, and it includes several natural vegetation zones. Among these are mist-shrouded cloudforest and elfin woodland

found in the cool and extremely wet conditions above 900 metres (3,000 feet) and dominated by mosses, ferns and lichen-encrusted stunted trees. There are also important tracts of montane rainforest, in a narrow altitudinal zone in which Dominica's only native conifer, *Podocarpus coriaceus*, grows. At lower elevations there is mature rainforest, in which the dominant tree species include the Amanoa *Amanoa caribaea*, the Candlewood or Gommier *Dacryodes excelsa* (the fruits and seeds of which are popular sources of food for birds, including parrots) and species of Chataignier or Breakaxe *Sloanea* spp., so called because of their very tough wood.

Overall, the rainforests of Dominica are estimated to support over 1,000 species of flowering plant, with around 60 woody plant and tree species per hectare (24 per acre). They are also home to two of the largest mammals found in the West Indies: the Antillean Agouti *Dasyprocta antillensis* and the Manicou or Opossum *Didelphis marsupialis*. Both species are essentially animals of the South American mainland and were introduced to Dominica several centuries ago (or possibly longer) by native Amerindians. The forests also harbour one of the world's largest frogs, the bizarrely named Dominican Mountain Chicken *Leptodactylus fallax*, so called because its highly prized flesh is said to taste like chicken. In recent years the numbers of this iconic creature, which is known locally as the Crapaud and even appears on Dominica's coat

BELOW **Much of the island of Montserrat has been covered by lava, ash and mud produced by ongoing volcanic activity. The area of rainforest has been reduced as a result, and the population of Montserrat Oriole affected accordingly.**

of arms, have crashed as a result of the fungal disease chytridiomycosis, which has killed 70 per cent or so of the population since the first outbreak on the island in 2002. To try and protect the species it is now illegal to hunt or eat Crapauds, and research is under way into a disease that is continuing to have a serious impact on amphibian populations worldwide.

Two other important areas of West Indian rainforest are to be found on St Lucia: the Edmund Forest Reserve and the Quillesse Rainforest Reserve. The former covers 7,700 hectares (19,000 acres), with areas of primary and secondary forest, rich in orchids and bromeliads, as well as plantations of various species managed for their commercial value. These include Blue Mahoe *Hibiscus elatus*, Caribbean Pine *Pinus caribaea*, Gmelina *Gmelina arborea*, Honduras Mahogany *Swietenia macrophylla* and *Leucaeana leucocephala*. As on many Caribbean islands, there is a substantial number of non-native plants growing in the forest here, including trees such as African Tulip *Spathodea campanulata* and Screw Pine *Pandanus utilis*. Trails through the forest provide dramatic views of the sea and the island's highest peak, Mount Gimie, as well as the opportunity to see several of St Lucia's endemic bird species, among them St Lucia Blackfinch *Melanospiza richardsoni*, St Lucia Oriole *Icterus laudabilis*, St Lucia Pewee *Contopus oberi*, St Lucia Warbler *Dendroica delicata* and Forest Thrush *Cichlherminia lherminieri*. These species are also present in the Quillesse Forest Reserve, which, although smaller in extent than the Edmund Forest Reserve, is arguably the most pristine of St Lucia's surviving rainforest and the most highly rated spot on the island among birdwatchers.

St Lucia's most high profile endemic bird is undoubtedly the St Lucia Parrot *Amazona versicolor*, whose fortunes have mirrored those of its Imperial cousin on Dominica. By the 1970s the hunting of this bird for food and trapping for the cagebird trade, together with the depletion across much of the island of its rainforest home (of which only 25 per cent or so survives), had reduced its numbers to a very low ebb. Subsequent conservation measures have been successful and the population now stands at 400–500 birds, although the opportunity for numbers to grow further is now restricted by a lack of suitable habitat. The parrot's forest home continues to be at risk from the development and expansion of agricultural plantations, as well as from residential construction, but there is now a strong emphasis on conservation and the development of ecotourism on the island is providing economic opportunities that should help boost rainforest conservation. Ironically, St Lucia is home to Papa Bois, the so-called "Father of the Forest", an evil spirit who traditionally led hunters and woodcutters to their death in revenge for their predations on his rainforest domain.

The vulnerability of island wildlife, not just to the activities of man but also to natural phenomena, has been brought into sharp focus by events since 1995 on the small island of Montserrat. In July that year the previously dormant Soufrière Hills volcano erupted with great ferocity, resulting in the devastation of the capital, Plymouth, the evacuation of most of the island's human population and the destruction of large areas of rainforest, which had previously covered up to 70 per cent of the island. Volcanic activity has continued to this day, albeit on a reduced scale, but lava flows, ash falls and acid rain have destroyed over half of the forest habitat of one of the world's rarest and most localized birds, the endemic Montserrat Oriole *Icterus oberi*. Its population has declined sharply as a result, even in those areas of forest seemingly unaffected by the eruption. Also struggling to survive is one of the world's only two populations of Mountain Chicken (once found on several other Caribbean islands but now restricted to Montserrat and Dominica), which is even less well equipped than the oriole to escape the impact of lava, ash and mudflows. Both species are now on a knife edge – one more natural calamity, such as a hurricane or a resurgence in the volcanic activity – could see them move into extinction in the wild.

ABOVE **With the forests on its island home under continuing threat from natural forces, a successful captive breeding programme for the Montserrat Oriole at Jersey Zoo should at least mean that the species is safe from total extinction.**

18. The Valdivian Rainforests of Southern Chile

The coastal rainforests of southern Chile are the only temperate rainforests in South America. Although much depleted by logging and clearance for agriculture, they remain the world's second most extensive area of woodland of that type, after those found in the western United States and Canada. The Chilean or Valdivian rainforests evolved following the retreat of glaciers some 10,000 years ago, eventually cloaking the slopes of the coastal cordillera and extending into the Andean valleys up to an altitude of 1,000 metres (3,000 feet) or so. Their character is determined by the generally cool and wet climatic conditions that occur here throughout the year, with annual rainfall totalling more than 5 metres (16 feet) in some locations, and with modest temperatures and a high incidence of cloud cover at all seasons. Forming a closed-canopy environment drenched in rain and humidity and luxuriant in mosses and ferns, these forests include extensive stands of deciduous trees, unlike the temperate rainforests of North America, which are almost exclusively coniferous in character.

OPPOSITE **Many of the more accessible estuaries and river valleys have been largely stripped of their large native trees. One needs to go further inland, or climb, to find tracts of relatively pristine forest that still contain mature Alerces and other indigenous species.**

RIGHT **Where unaffected by logging and clearance, the temperate rainforests of Chile have a lush understorey and forest floor. The profusion of mosses, lichens and ferns supports many species of invertebrate.**

ABOVE **The Puma is the largest predator in Chile's temperate rainforests. Overall population density is low, and the animals range widely in search of prey. They will take anything from small rodents to large deer.**

At lower elevations the Valdivian forests are often dominated by types of Southern Beech *Nothofagus* spp., particularly Coihue *N. dombeyi*, which can reach a height of 50 metres (165 feet), as well as other tree species such as Tepa *Laureliopsis philippiana*, Olivillo *Aextoxicon punctatum*, Luma *Amomyrtus luma* (a fragrant evergreen) and the beautiful summer-blooming Ulmo *Eucryphia cordifolia*, its conspicuous white flowers a dramatic contrast against the dark green foliage around. These forests were largely intact at the time of the initial European "discovery" of Chile in the sixteenth century, but increasing settlement during the subsequent three centuries has had a disastrous impact. The more accessible forests, mainly those at lower elevations, were extensively cleared for their timber and to make way for farmland, despite the fact that the resulting clear-felled land was often too wet to be productive agriculturally (even as pasture) and was subsequently abandoned. Today, only about 40 per cent of the temperate rainforests extant in Chile at the time of European contact still survive. Their story is mirrored in the particular fate of one of the most notable tree species they support: the mighty Alerce or Patagonian Cypress *Fitzroya cupressoides*.

The Alerce is endemic to southern Chile and parts of western Argentina, its range originally extending from 39–43°S in the coastal mountains south of Valdivia south to the area around the Michinmahido Volcano and eastwards into the valleys on the Argentinian slopes of the Andes. It is the only extant member of its genus, which was named after Captain Robert Fitzroy, who sailed *HMS Beagle* and naturalist Charles Darwin along this part of the Chilean coast in the 1830s. With mature trees exceeding 55 metres (180 feet) in height and with trunks in excess of 5 metres (16 feet) in diameter, this member of the cypress family is the undisputed monarch

of the Valdivian rainforests and understandably often referred to as the "Redwood of South America". Extremely slow growing (an average tree will grow about 1 centimetre/0.4 inches every 15 years), it is longer-lived than either of its two more famous relatives, the Coast or California Redwood *Sequoia sempervirens* and the Giant Sequoia *Sequoiadendron giganteum* of the western United States. Analysis of a large Alerce stump in 1993 revealed that the tree had lived for 3,622 years, and a few specimens of similar, or even older, vintage still survive. Only one other tree species – the Bristlecone Pine *Pinus longaeva* of the Great Basin in the west-central United States – has been reliably documented as living for longer than the Alerce.

Today, what were once extensive tracts of Alerces are highly fragmented, with hardly any specimens remaining at the more accessible lower elevations and with many surviving stands in degraded condition. The high resin content in Alerce wood makes it resistant to decomposition and rot, and so it was always popular for construction and for external use, such as for roof shingles. The oldest and largest Alerces were felled for their timber in the nineteenth and twentieth centuries, among them individuals that were probably over 4,000 years old and certainly with a trunk girth in excess of 7 or 8 metres (23–26 feet). In 1976 a Chilean presidential decree prohibited the felling of Alerces, which were declared a national monument. The rate of destruction slowed dramatically, but although only dead Alerce wood can legally be removed from the forest, illicit felling of live trees still goes on. Alerces are also vulnerable to the collateral damage caused by the logging of other species around them and by the replacement of native trees with exotic species of pine and eucalyptus. Infrastructural development, especially

ABOVE One of the smallest ungulates, the Southern Pudu stands only 35 centimetres or so (13.7 inches) at the shoulder. It tends to stay deep within thick forest, occasionally emerging from cover to feed in more open terrain, usually at dusk.

LEFT Few trees are as majestic as an old Alerce. Very slow growing, an average Alerce will take several hundred years to reach maturity and more than two thousand before it can be regarded as a true "veteran". Sadly the oldest and biggest trees of all were felled for their timber during the nineteenth and twentieth centuries.

road construction, is a further threat, as are the prospecting and exploitation of minerals.

It is estimated that only 15 per cent or so of the original Alerce forests survive, most of these at more inaccessible higher elevations. As many as one-third of the world's remaining Alerces can be found in Pumalin Park, 300,000 hectares (750,000 acres) of protected land in Palena province, including important tracts of undisturbed temperate rainforest. Sections of the forest were first acquired by American businessman Doug Tompkins in the early 1990s to protect them from logging, and have since been added to by the California-based Conservation Land Trust. Essentially a "private" national park, Pumalin Park was declared a nature sanctuary by the Chilean government in 2001. Some 20,000 hectares (50,000 acres) of Alerce forest are contained with the Alerce Andino National Park, east of Puerto Montt, and groves of mature Alerces in good condition can also be found in the Cochamó Valley, further to the east and at the southern end of Chile's "Lake District". Although the majestic trees that were once found here along the Estuario Reconquavi have long been cut down, some of the best Alerces in Chile can be found higher up in the valley, particularly in the La Junta area, where they are accessible only via steep trails.

The Valdivian rainforests support a wealth of specialized wildlife, including iconic species that are dependent on extensive tracts of mature woodland. Among these is the Magellanic

Woodpecker *Campephilus magellanicus*, South America's largest woodpecker and a vulnerable member of a depleted genus, following the presumed recent extinction in Mexico of the Imperial Woodpecker *C. imperialis* and the doubt now cast on the alleged rediscovery of the extinct Ivory-billed Woodpecker *C. principalis* in the United States in 2004 (although the Cuban race of this species may still survive). Another significant resident is the Rufous-legged Owl *Strix rufipes*, which occupies a similar ecological niche to the Northern Spotted Owl *Strix occidentalis caurina*, the great conservation *cause célèbre* of the temperate rainforests of the Pacific coast of the United States (see page 108). Forest mammals include Puma *Puma concolor*, widely distributed but very difficult to see, the endangered Huemul (*Hippocamelus bisulcus*), a species of deer highly dependent on the forest during winter and whose numbers have fallen dramatically following the destruction and fragmentation of its habitat, and the Southern or Chilean Pudu *Pudu puda*, the smallest deer species in the world.

The wildlife importance of the temperate rainforest ecosystem was one of the motivations behind the acquisition and inauguration (in 2005) of the Valdivian Coastal Reserve, 59,700 hectares (147,500 acres) of rainforest immediately south of the city of Valdivia. Previously held by a logging company, but now owned and managed by The Nature Conservancy and other conservation organizations, including input from the World Wide Fund for Nature, the reserve protects important areas of Alerces, as well as some of the most extensive surviving stands of Olivillo trees anywhere in Chile. The restoration of plantations of non-native species to indigenous forest is already in hand, as are initiatives aimed at perpetuating traditional land-use patterns and developing sustainable ecotourism within appropriate areas of the reserve. However, the majority of Chile's temperate rainforests remains outside protected areas and must be regarded as vulnerable to further degradation and destruction. The fact that these are among the most magical places anywhere in the world makes their predicament all the more poignant. The special quality of the Valdivian rainforest environment was epitomized by the celebrated writer Pablo Neruda in his *Memoirs* (1977): "Anyone who hasn't been in the Chilean forest doesn't know this planet".

LEFT **Magellanic Woodpeckers require both a large territory and mature trees in which to excavate their nest-holes. Like all large woodpecker species across the world, they have suffered from the selective removal of the largest trees in many forests.**

LEFT The dramatic scenery of the Valdivian rainforest makes it a popular destination with those interested in outdoor pursuits, especially hiking. The support of such groups has reinforced the arguments of those campaigning for these forests to be better protected from insensitive exploitation and development.

19. The Canopy Tower and Soberania National Park, Panama

Waking up in the rainforest is a magical experience. To have one's first glimpse of the new day as the first shafts of light rake across the horizon and hit the treetops is a real privilege. This is the moment at which the rainforest can appear at its most immense and overwhelming and yet paradoxically at its most intimate, as the creatures that live within it begin to stir and rapidly bring the canopy to life as the sky brightens. Watching this process unfold is all the more special when you are actually up in the canopy, an experience which is possible in Panama's world-famous Canopy Tower, one of the best places in the world for observing rainforest birds.

Now converted to an eco-lodge offering superlative wildlife watching, the tower started life in 1965 as a radar station built on the top of the 275-metre (900-foot) high Semaphore Hill and used by the United States Air Force to help control the airspace over the Panama Canal. It was taken out of commission some years later but remained in American hands until 1996, when it was transferred to the Panamanian authorities. Today it offers the opportunity to view a vast number of forest canopy birds that are normally difficult to see well. Many of them are attracted to the lodge's feeders, providing astonishing views, down to a few metres, of dramatic canopy species such as cotingas, motmots and toucans. The tower is also an excellent point from which to observe birds in flight, not only residents such as parrots but also migratory species, especially raptors like Broad-winged and Swainson's Hawks, *Buteo platypterus* and *B. swainsoni*, which pass through in spring and autumn in their thousands en route to and from North America. At peak times the visible migration from the tower is staggering in terms of the numbers involved.

Breakfasting with the birds is not the only reason for visiting Soberania National Park. The park covers 19,341 hectares (47,792 acres) of prime lowland rainforest, much of it immediately adjacent to the Panama Canal, and in terms of pure accessibility it is hard to beat – just a 25-minute drive

OPPOSITE Toucan species, such as this Keel-billed Toucan *Ramphastos sulfuratus*, are a common sight from the Canopy Tower. They usually move around in small groups, flying from tree to tree in search of food.

BELOW Soberania National Park is an outstanding area for wildlife and a reminder of the rainforest that once covered much of lowland Central America. Biodiversity levels are very high here, and the park's avifauna in particular is well studied.

north-west from the skyscrapers of Panama City. The forest here is generally in very good condition and highly diverse. The large number of mature trees include majestic examples of Amarillo *Terminalia amazonica*, one of the tallest trees in the forest and rising above the main canopy to heights of 40 metres (130 feet) and more, Cotton Tree *Ceiba pentandra*, Cuipo *Cavanillesia platanifolia*, another one of the forest's most distinctive emergents, Guarumo *Cecropia obtusifolia*, much favoured by sloths, and Guayacan *Tabebuia guayacan*, famous for its brightly coloured flowers. There is an impressive supporting cast of epiphytes and orchids.

The park supports over 100 mammal species and at least 70 species of reptile. Although the neotropical rainforest's top predator, the Jaguar *Panthera onca*, is reported still to occur here, visitors stand a much greater, if still modest, chance of seeing the Jaguar's smaller relative, the Ocelot *Leopardus pardalis*. Views of this delightful small cat are most likely along the streams and small watercourses, where its distinctive tracks should be looked for. More readily on view are primates such as Mantled Howler Monkey *Alouatta palliata*, Geoffrey's Tamarin *Saguinus geoffroyi* and White-throated Capuchin *Cebus capucinus*, all of which can be seen from the Canopy Tower with luck and patience. White-nosed Coatis *Nasua narica* are often seen foraging along the tracks and trails, and other mammals include sloths (both Two-toed *Choloepus hoffmanni* and Three-toed *Bradypus variegatus* are present), White-tailed Deer *Odocoileus virginianus*, and one of the most enchanting of all forest animals, the Northern Tamandua *Tamandua mexicana*. This distinctive species of anteater is as much at home on the ground as up in the trees, where it will search for the nests of ants, termites and bees. It eagerly tears the nests apart with its massive claws before feasting on the inhabitants, and the noise produced by this breaking-and-entering can be an effective aid in

BELOW **Part of the park runs directly along the side of the Panama Canal and includes the last sections of the canal's banks to retain their natural vegetation. Gallery forest such as this is particularly good for birdlife.**

OPPOSITE TOP **Geoffrey's Tamarins are regularly seen from the Canopy Tower. Feeding on insects, fruit and leaves, they move through the trees in small groups of up to twelve or so, communicating with each other via a range of birdlike calls.**

OPPOSITE BOTTOM **During the wet season the Northern Tamandua feeds mainly on ants, shifting during the dry season to termites, which have a higher moisture content. Such seasonal changes in animal behaviour remain an imperfectly understood aspect of the rainforest ecosystem.**

locating a feeding Tamandua up in the canopy. On the ground they appear rather clumsy and slow, perhaps hampered in the lower light levels by their poor eyesight.

Whereas the Tamandua is both diurnal and nocturnal, one other interesting mammal often seen in Soberania is much more of a night creature – the Kinkajou *Potus flavus*. This fruit-eater is very much an animal of the canopy, hardly ever (if at all) seen on the ground, and usually found where there are fruiting trees, especially figs. In such locations Kinkajous can be quite common, and although usually encountered singly or in pairs, they will sometime gather in small groups where food is particularly plentiful, often dangling from a branch by their prehensile tail to reach a particularly attractive fruit. They are agile animals, running and leaping between trees like monkeys, but are hard to see well, owing to their nocturnal habits; when they are seen in daylight, this is usually when a night of heavy rain has prevented them from feeding.

The cover of darkness also offers the chance of finding one of Soberania's real mammalian specialities, Rothschild's Porcupine *Coendou rothschildi*. This secretive creature is endemic to Panama and is regularly reported from the forests around the Canopy Tower. Completely arboreal, it has a long prehensile tail with which to secure itself when foraging for food in the treetops.

Such mammal highlights notwithstanding, it is for its birds that most visitors come to Soberania and especially to the Canopy Tower. The tower gives excellent views over the surrounding forest and well-stocked birdfeeders ensure superb views of bird species that are otherwise difficult to see well. However tempting it may be to stay put, some of the best birding is to had along the network of roads and trails leading from the tower, such as the road up Semaphore Hill to the tower itself and the Plantation Trail, which gives access to a former cocoa, coffee and rubber plantation that came out of production in the early 1900s and has since reverted to secondary forest rich in birds. However, perhaps the most famous birding strip is along the Pipeline Road, which runs for 17 kilometres (10 miles) across the park. This is the area where the local Audubon Society holds an annual Christmas bird count, which on one day in December 1992 logged 525 species, a world record for the total number seen in a 24-hour period.

Wherever one chooses to go birding here, one of the forest features to look out for is a swarm of ants *Eciton* spp. When on the move, these will always attract a range of interesting bird species, notably antbirds, antshrikes, antvireos and antwrens (members of the Thamnophilidae family). The 200-plus individual species in this group are so named because of their habit of locating and then closely associating with the vanguard of an ant swarm, feeding on the insects and other creatures

OPPOSITE **Commonly mistaken for a type of monkey, the nocturnal Kinkajou's closest relatives are actually the raccoons and coatis. Kinkajous have few natural enemies, as they are usually out of reach of terrestrial predators and their nocturnal habits keep them safe from diurnal airborne threats such as Harpy Eagles.**

BELOW **This is one of the few photographs ever taken of a Rothschild's Porcupine in the wild. A shy, canopy-dwelling creature, it feeds mainly on fruit.**

BELOW **One of the great rainforest birding experiences is to encounter an ant swarm with various antbirds in attendance. Usually totally engrossed in feasting on the ants, these often shy birds can give superb views in such circumstances. This is an Ocellated Antbird *Phaenostictus mcleannani*.**

that are flushed out by the aggressive ants. Sizeable flocks of birds can gather on such occasions, numbering as many as 20–30 different species. This makes for exciting birding, as many of these species are shy and retiring, normally confining themselves to the darkest corners of the understorey and almost invariably being heard rather than seen. Ant swarms offer the rare chance to observe them out in the open.

The park contains some interesting historical sites, notably 9.5 kilometres (6 miles) of the famous Camino de Cruces, a cobblestone road constructed in the sixteenth century by the Spanish using slave labour, and which ran for 80 kilometres (50 miles) through the forest. Its purpose was to transport gold and other treasure safely from the Pacific coast to ships waiting in the Caribbean, the goods being carried by mule trains through what was then exceedingly difficult terrain. Foremost among Soberania's non-wildlife attractions is undoubtedly the Panama Canal – the park runs along a substantial section of the eastern bank of this extraordinary feat of engineering, and visitors are regularly confronted with the bizarre sight of huge ships seemingly cleaving their way through the forest as they move along the out-of-view canal. As the last wooded section along the canal's banks, the forest here has an important practical function, in that the high density of trees helps prevent soil erosion and the undesirable build-up of silt.

Although the very accessibility of Soberania and the Canopy Tower has helped secure their well-deserved profile for excellent birding and a top rainforest "experience", the very fact that the park is so close to Panama City brings a range of pressures as well as opportunities. Infrastructural encroachment on the forest is growing – highways already cut across the edges of the park, and with the city suburbs creeping ever closer, issues such as the illegal dumping of refuse and the contamination of watercourses from industrial and agricultural activity are increasing sources of concern. The absence of a designated buffer zone, which could serve to alleviate direct pressure on the park and its wildlife, is a major problem. However, projects directed at community involvement in aspects such as agroforestry, reforestation and ecotourism offer hope for the future.

LEFT The accessibility of Soberania makes it a popular weekend destination with the city-dwellers of Panama City. Growing urban encroachment is one of a range of issues facing the authorities, but the park and the Canopy Tower are ideally placed to serve as an educational focus for rainforest conservation.

OPPOSITE Three-toed Sloths can sometimes be spotted from the Canopy Tower. These remarkable creatures spend almost all of their time up in the treetops, only descending to the ground to defecate (roughly once per week).

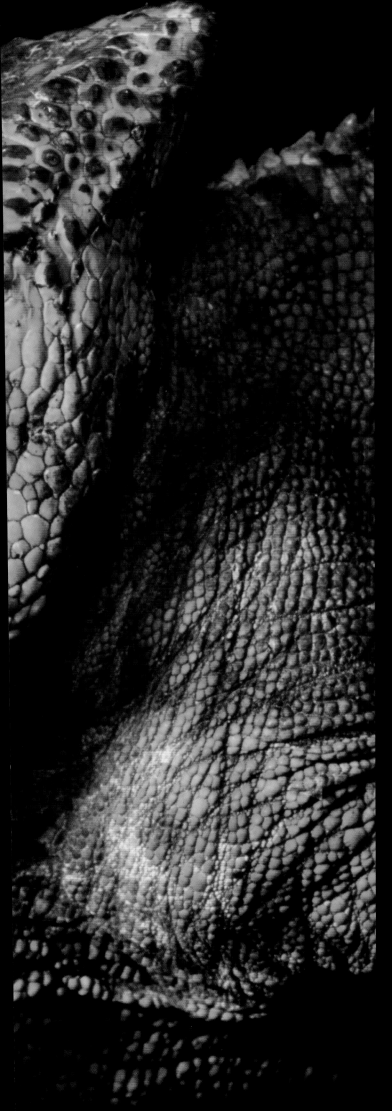

AFRICA

Swathes of dense rainforest still cover much of equatorial Africa, from Senegal in the far west to the fringes of the Indian Ocean in the east. In the middle of the continent lies the Congo Basin, home to the second-largest expanse of tropical rainforest in the world. Still relatively unexplored by scientists, much of this green heart of Africa remains cloaked in dense vegetation and serves as a refuge to some of the largest surviving populations of iconic African animals, such as the elephant and lowland gorilla. To the east lie the mountains of the Great Rift, their slopes supporting tracts of montane rainforest and cloudforest, rich in flora and birds, as well as providing home to the last few hundred mountain gorillas. In East Africa, isolated uplands – so-called "sky islands" – support species so restricted in range that they may inhabit an area only a few square kilometres in extent. This vulnerability is now all the more apparent, as rainforest across the continent is under increasing pressure from logging, hunting and agricultural expansion.

LEFT One of the most distinctive types of lizard, chameleons are widely distributed across Africa, with many species represented in the rainforest environment. They are noted for a range of interesting features, not least their extraordinarily long tongue, which can exceed their body length.

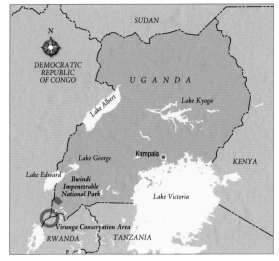

20. The Mountain Gorillas of Bwindi Impenetrable Forest, Uganda

Although relatively modest in size – a mere 331 square kilometres (128 square miles) – this aptly named tract of montane rainforest is of paramount conservation importance, thanks to its role as home to almost half of the world's 720 or so surviving Mountain Gorillas *Gorilla berengei berengei*. First protected as a forest reserve in 1932, Bwindi was upgraded to national park status in 1991 and declared a World Heritage Site three years later. Today the park is one of Uganda's most popular destinations for tourists, almost all of whom are attracted by the prospect of visiting one of the habituated groups of gorillas that live here.

Located in the Kigezi Highlands on the edge of the western arm of Africa's Great Rift Valley, Bwindi is a remnant of much larger tracts of rainforest that once extended right along the Rift escarpment and south to the Virunga volcanoes (home to the other Mountain Gorilla populations). Their clearance by both nomadic pastoralists and more sedentary agriculturalists began at least 1,500 years ago, and the forests became increasingly fragmented – Bwindi was probably separated from the Virunga forests, for example, by about the fifteenth century. However, the area's human population remained relatively low until the late nineteenth century, when large numbers of farmers moved into the area and began clearing the remaining areas of forest to establish agricultural plots. The rate of destruction continued until relatively recently,

RIGHT The terrain across much of the Impenetrable Forest is very steep, the vegetation as dense as the park's name suggests. This inaccessibility has helped protect the area's wildlife, particularly its population of endangered Mountain Gorillas.

OPPOSITE Surely one of the most magnificent of all animals, a silverback Mountain Gorilla. Chest-thumping notwithstanding, gorillas are essentially peaceable creatures and conflict is much rarer in gorilla society than with chimpanzees, for example.

itself symptomatic of the wider natural habitat destruction that is occurring as a result of Uganda's burgeoning population requiring more and more resources to sustain itself.

The mostly iron-rich soils of Bwindi make for poor farmland, however. Generally acidic in nature and of weak composition, they break down easily in dry weather and erode at an alarming rate once stripped of their vegetative cover and exposed to the elements. Crop yields and productivity are therefore rather low and of limited viability and duration on any one plot. Most local people are subsistence farmers, eking out a living on the meagre terraces they or their ancestors have carved from the precipitous slopes. Some groups were, however, once able to live in a more sustainable balance with the forest environment and its wildlife. Notable among these are the Batwa, hunter-gatherers who lived traditionally within the forest and obtained most, if not all, of their needs from forest products. Particularly skilled at hunting and the collection of honey, they were ejected from what was then the Bwindi Game Reserve in the 1960s, and have since lived as landless labourers and farmers around the park's periphery.

In terms of topography, the park ranges in altitude from 1,160 metres (3,800 feet) to a peak of 2,607 metres (8,551 feet) and is mostly composed of steep ridges and narrow valley bottoms. Only one small section is flat – an area of swamp, particularly significant for its birdlife. The park is a critically important water catchment area for this part of Uganda, and as the source of five major rivers it is responsible for 75 per cent or more of the run-off that feeds into Lake Edward, to the north. The hydrological balance of the whole region therefore depends on the park, its very presence helping to determine local weather patterns and in particular to boost rainfall levels. Typical Bwindi weather is cool and cloudy, with mists a frequent occurrence at the beginning and the end of the day. Rainfall averages 1,450 millimetres (57 inches) per annum, distributed between two main rainy seasons, March–April and September–November.

Most of the park consists of thick forest, containing at least 200 indigenous species of tree (including at least 12 endemics), with Grey Plum *Parinari excelsa* one of the commoner species at lower elevations and others such as *Chrysophyllum gorungosanum* prevailing higher up. The valleys are particularly diverse, with tree ferns (*Cyathea* spp.) especially notable, and it is here also that some of the tallest trees grow, among them *Newtonia buchananii* and *Croton megalocarpus*. On the hill slopes species such as African Olive *Olea capensis* and Pillarwood *Cassipourea malosana* predominate, while the windy and exposed ridge-tops support communities of dwarf vegetation. The closed canopy nature of much of the forest makes life difficult for herbaceous vegetation down below, but fern species (*Pteridium* spp.) thrive in the shady conditions and there are also a few areas of Mountain Bamboo *Arundinaria alpina*.

Fruiting trees such as Grey Plum and Giant Yellow Mulberry *Myrianthus holstii* are important food sources for Bwindi's populations of primates. Several species of monkey are present in the park, the most common and regularly recorded being the two races of Blue Monkey, *Cercopithecus mitis stuhlmanni* and *C. m. doggetti*, which interbreed here, and the Redtail Monkey *Cercopithecus ascanius*. Also present are l'Hoest's Monkey *Cercopithecus lhoesti* and Black and White Colobus *Colobus guereza*, as well as Olive Baboon *Papio anubis* and Chimpanzee *Pan troglodytes*. However, none of these species is particularly easy to see at Bwindi and they are, in any case, totally overshadowed by the park's main draw: its world-famous population of Mountain Gorillas.

LEFT Forest birding at Bwindi is particularly rewarding, as many West African species have their only East African toehold here. Among the more obvious birds are the brightly coloured turacos, including the striking Ross's Turaco *Musophaga rossae*.

RIGHT The opportunity to watch gorilla family life at first hand is one of the main attractions at Bwindi. Human access is carefully regulated to ensure there is no undue disturbance and, if one of the habituated gorilla groups shows signs of repeated unease, then "visits" are suspended.

OPPOSITE **Young gorillas are highly adventurous, constantly exploring their environment and always experimenting with whatever comes to hand. Gorillas usually give birth to just one baby, which will take between two and a half and three years to be fully weaned. During this period the infant mortality can be as high as 40 per cent.**

Bwindi's gorillas have been studied by scientists for over thirty years and visited by tourists on an organized basis since 1991. A census in 2006 revealed that the park supports some 340 individual gorillas (a slight increase on the 2002 census figure), mostly divided into 30 family groups but including at least 10 solitary males. Five groups are currently habituated to tourism. Access to these groups is strictly controlled through an expensive permit system and by a daily restriction on the number of visitors allowed to visit each group. The behaviour of the visitors when close to the gorillas is also subject to various conditions, such safeguards being essential to protect the animals from excessive disturbance as well as from human-borne diseases such as the common cold, which can be fatal to gorillas. As a result, it is possible to watch wild gorillas at close quarters, behaving naturally and without fear of man – undoubtedly one of the most remarkable and moving of all wildlife experiences.

Mountain Gorillas differ from their lowland counterparts in that they have longer, thicker hair, broader chests and bulkier jaws, and in appearance the Bwindi population – which lives in mid-elevation forest – is intermediate between the mountain gorillas of the Virungas, which live at higher altitude, and the lowland gorillas that inhabit the lower-altitude forests to the west. In habits they are all broadly similar, spending 60 per cent of their time foraging and feeding and the remaining 40 per cent at rest. At Bwindi the gorillas live in family groups of 10–12 members on average, although groups of over 30 have been recorded. Only groups of between six and 15 animals are considered suitable for habituation to tourism.

ABOVE **Blue Monkeys are common and widespread in the forest at Bwindi, with the interbreeding of two different races giving rise to many different colour variations. They usually move around in troops comprising one male and roughly 10 females and young.**

The process of habituation can take up to two years. It begins with the park trackers and rangers attempting to locate a family group on a daily basis, then sitting quietly in the forest near them for hours at a time, at first out of sight, whilst making calming vocalizations so that the gorillas both become used to the human presence and also reassured that they are under no threat. After a few months, the gorillas usually become more relaxed and will start to feed more readily in the open, in full view of their human observers and often allowing an approach to within a few metres. The behaviour of any family group is always contingent upon the lead taken by the silverback male, so his attitude is critical.

Gorilla-tracking is a lucrative form of wildlife tourism for Uganda, as well as for Rwanda and the Democratic Republic of Congo, where habituated gorillas can also be visited, although the number of visitors to the DRC has fallen sharply in recent years as a result of political instability. Sadly, habituating gorillas to human presence is not without risk; a silverback, pregnant female and two breeding-age females, all of which were used to humans and did not see them as a threat, were massacred by renegade soldiers in Virunga National Park in July 2007. For this reason the vast majority of Mountain Gorillas are left free of human contact and, while their overall numbers continue to show a slight increase, their long-term future remains precarious. Habitat loss has meant that opportunities for their potential expansion are acutely limited; in Rwanda, for example, the habituated groups live within a relatively small island of habitat entirely surrounded by farmland, and gorilla-watching there sometimes takes place against a backdrop of local villagers calling to each other as they plant or gather their crops just a few hundred metres below. This telling juxtaposition serves to underline how fragile the Mountain Gorilla's situation has become.

ABOVE **Adolescent gorillas spend much of their time watching their parents and learning the social skills and understanding of group hierarchy that are essential for adult life. At puberty almost all males leave their natal group; three-quarters of females do likewise.**

RIGHT **Although well protected, Bwindi Impenetrable Forest is hemmed in by a sea of farmland. Deforested slopes, scoured of their vegetation and often burnt before cultivation starts, are a stark reminder of the fate of many thousands of square kilometres of rainforest across much of Africa in recent years.**

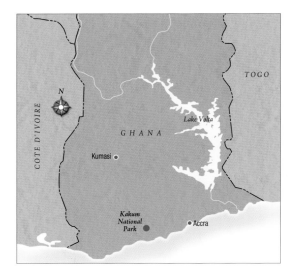

21. West Africa's Rainforest Fragments: Kakum National Park, Ghana

At the turn of the twentieth century, dense lowland rainforest extended in an almost unbroken swathe across West Africa, from western Sierra Leone eastwards to the border of Ghana and Togo. Covering some 1.27 million square kilometres (488,000 square miles) and spanning what are now six countries, in some places this forest ran continuously from the coast inland for over 300 kilometres (185 miles). It harboured a bewildering wealth of wildlife, including many thousands of elephants and buffalo and some of the world's most interesting primates. Yet today barely 15 per cent of this rainforest survives, broken into scattered fragments. These are under intense pressure and continuing to dwindle, with little more than 10 per cent of the surviving forest currently protected.

Known to ecologists as the Upper Guinean Forest zone, this is one of the most biodiverse regions of Africa and particularly important for mammals – almost half of the continent's species occur here. One of the most important surviving tracts of this once vast forest is Kakum National Park in southern Ghana. Kakum first became a protected area in 1932 in an attempt to save it from uncontrolled hunting, logging and destruction in favour of farmland. With the contiguous Assin Atandaso Resource Reserve it now protects 357 square kilometres (138 square miles) of rainforest, much of which was logged from the mid-1970s until the late 1980s. The park therefore includes extensive areas of regenerating secondary forest, but there are also important sectors of primary forest with a well-developed canopy and relatively clear understorey – a reminder of the type of mature forest that once covered almost the entire region.

Among the main attractions at Kakum is undoubtedly the impressive canopy walkway, the only one in Africa and erected some 40 metres (130 feet) above the forest floor. Running for 360 metres (1,180 feet) through the canopy, suspended walkways secured by steel cables link a series of

OPPOSITE **Immediately recognizable from its familiar role as a talking pet, the Grey Parrot has declined across much of its range as a result of excessive trapping for the pet trade. Protective legislation is routinely flouted in many African countries and baby Greys are sadly a common sight in markets.**

RIGHT **For many visitors Kakum's canopy walkway is the park's main highlight. It gives a superb insight into life in the canopy, but equally rewarding are expeditions on foot along the forest trails down below.**

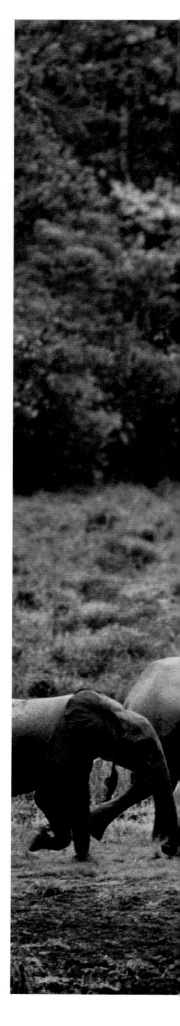

platforms mounted in large trees. Panic attacks and vertigo notwithstanding, the walkway – and, perhaps more comfortably, the platforms – offer stupendous views into the forest canopy and the chance to see birds and animals that are normally only glimpsed indistinctly from down below and which rarely, if ever, descend to ground level. These include avian specialities such as Forest Wood-hoopoe *Phoeniculus castaneiceps* and Yellow-billed or Verreaux's Turaco *Tauraco macrorhynchus* both regular here, as well as several species of hornbill (see below) and raptors such as African Harrier-Hawk *Polyboroides typus*, Cassin's Hawk-Eagle *Spizaetus africanus* and Red-chested Goshawk *Accipiter toussenelii*. Usually only seen when soaring high above the forest, these impressive birds of prey can sometimes be spotted from the walkway as they perch quietly in the tops of the larger trees. Butterflies, of which over 550 species have been recorded at Kakum, are also outstanding.

As in all rainforests, birding in Kakum can be a testing affair. Although over 270 species of bird have been recorded in the park and immediate area (with at least a further 50 likely to occur here), and the canopy walkway is one of the best birding locations in the whole of West Africa, the avian action is often quite concentrated and heavily dependent on time of day and weather. It is important to be out early, as bird activity is markedly reduced by mid-morning and the middle of the day can be very quiet before a second "wave" in the two hours or so before sunset. Early morning is certainly the best time to see one of Kakum's flagship species, the African Grey Parrot *Psittacus erithacus*. Heavily depleted in numbers across much of its range as a result of the illegal pet trade, there are still reasonable numbers of this charismatic species in Kakum and they are best seen shortly after dawn, when they head out from their overnight roosts in search of food, raucously screeching and displaying their bright red vents as they whirr overhead. Red-fronted Parrots *Poicephalus gulielmi* are also seen regularly.

One of the best strategies for birding in the forest is to stake out a fruiting tree, such as a species of fig. These act as magnets to a wide variety of fruit-eating birds, which will gather in considerable numbers in a particularly tempting and well-laden tree. Greenbuls, barbets and tinkerbirds are typical visitors, but the blue riband birds on such occasions are undoubtedly the hornbills. There are

ABOVE LEFT **Hornbills are common at Kakum, and even a short visit will give the opportunity to see two or three species. One of the most regularly seen is the African Pied Hornbill, which is able to live satisfactorily in secondary forest and even in agricultural plantations.**

ABOVE RIGHT **Although widely distributed across much of sub-Saharan Africa, the African Harrier-Hawk is nowhere common. It is highly omnivorous, and often seen scrambling along branches and across trunks, even dangling by its legs, whilst hunting for insects, eggs and young birds.**

OPPOSITE **West Africa's elephants are among the most secretive of their species. With their once large herds now broken into fragmented and declining populations, they have retreated to the remnants of their rainforest home.**

several species resident in the park and few birders leave without having seen at least some of them, most usually African Pied *Tockus fasciatus*, Black-casqued *Ceratogymna atrata* and Brown-cheeked *Bycanistes cylindricus*.

One former avian highlight of the park, but now almost certainly extinct here, is the White-breasted Guinea-fowl *Agelastes meleagrides*. This species is dependent on undisturbed primary rainforest with a closed canopy and relatively open forest floor, on which it forages for insects, fallen berries and seeds. Seemingly incapable of adapting to the dense growth typical of secondary forest, and heavily poached for its meat, the guineafowl is in rapid decline across its now seriously fragmented range, which includes parts of Côte d'Ivoire, Liberia and Sierra Leone. Very few are thought to be hanging on in Ghana.

Although known primarily for its outstanding birdlife, the park is also home to some interesting mammals, although these are not necessarily easy to see. An isolated population of some 250–300 Forest Elephants *Loxodonta cyclotis* lives here, the remnant of a once much larger population. With most of their habitat now destroyed and converted to farmland, the elephants are effectively corralled in the park and seriously restricted. Their traditional seasonal migratory routes are now impossible for them to follow, as the habitat is unsuitable, and their historical feeding grounds are also largely destroyed. In recent years they have come into increasing conflict with the farming communities that live adjacent to the park boundary. Immediately before harvest time, when crops are at their most tempting, the elephants would emerge from the forest under cover of darkness and raid the fields, causing extensive damage and destroying the livelihood of many families living barely at subsistence level. This understandably generated considerable antipathy towards the elephants on the part of local people and posed a major problem for the park authorities (and the elephants).

An ingenious solution was devised and has been successful at reducing the conflict between the elephants and the farmers. Elephants have an intense dislike of the scent of chilli peppers, and so cloths soaked in chilli oil are suspended from wires around the fields, to deter the elephants from entering the crops. This system also has the advantage of being cheaper and easier to set up than other elephant deterrents, such as electrified fences. However, the wider issue of how large-range mammals such as elephants are able to coexist satisfactorily alongside humans, and in "islands" of suitable habitat, continues to test conservationists and governments alike.

Few visitors to Kakum are lucky enough to see the park's generally elusive elephants, but most do see at least one or two species of monkey. At least six species are present here, and the canopy

LEFT The bushmeat trade is stripping many African rainforests of their wildlife. Heavy levels of indiscriminate trapping and shooting are having a serious impact on the populations of mammals and larger birds. Some species are now severely endangered and are likely to become extinct if the situation is not brought under control.

RIGHT The Yellow-backed Duiker is one of the most distinctive members of its family but hard to see well, as it usually keeps to dense stands of undergrowth. *Duiker* is the Afrikaans word for "diver", a reference to the way in which these animals plunge into thick cover.

walkway offers as rewarding a place to look for them as any. Most frequently seen are the Lesser Spot-nosed Monkey *Cercopithecus petaurista*, Mona Monkey *Cercopithecus mona* and Olive Colobus *Procolobus verus*. One very attractive primate, the Roloway Guenon *Cercopithecus diana roloway*, used to be found in the park but was eradicated by illegal hunting in the 1990s and may well be heading for global extinction. Other mammals include Western Tree Hyrax *Dendrohyrax dorsalis* (sometimes seen or heard from the canopy walkway), various species of squirrel, mongooses and duiker, notably Yellow-backed *Cephalophus sylvicultor*. Bongo *Tragelaphus euryceros* are alleged to live in the more remote parts of the forest, but are hardly ever seen and their continued presence must be in doubt.

Kakum is probably the best-protected forest site in Ghana and is outstanding for its birdlife, but sadly it is effectively an island in a sea of farmland. Even within its confines poaching continues to be a problem. The hunting of game for bushmeat has a long tradition in West Africa, and bushmeat has traditionally been an important source of protein for poorer people. The most popular quarry are larger birds, monkeys and small to medium-sized antelopes, such as duikers. In many places the "take" was historically sustainable, but in recent years the demand for bushmeat has soared, primarily as a result of increased popularity among city-dwellers and for an illegal export trade. No longer do local hunters shoot solely for their own pot, and as logging roads open up areas of forest that were hitherto relatively inaccessible, so the pressure on the animals there intensifies. In heavily shot areas, the result can be "empty forest syndrome", tracts of otherwise pristine forest in which wild animals are worryingly absent – all killed for bushmeat.

Pressure on the remnant rainforests of West Africa continues to intensify as human populations grow. Increasing desertification in the Sahel regions to the north of Ghana is fuelling a migration of subsistence farmers southwards, putting even greater strain on land resources in an already crowded environment. With demand for minerals and commodities such as tropical hardwoods still growing, the surviving fragments of the once magnificent Upper Guinean rainforest have never been in greater need of conservation attention and protection.

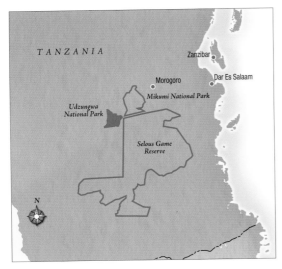

22. Tanzania's "Sky Islands": the Rainforests of the Udzungwas

Tanzania is without doubt one of the most exciting places for anyone interested in watching wildlife. Some of the greatest spectacles of the natural world are played out on the plains of the Serengeti, where vast numbers of ungulates and attendant predators have drawn outside visitors for over 100 years. Yet, impressive as they are, these herds are just one aspect of Tanzania's rich fauna, an outstanding biodiversity that extends well beyond the boundaries of the more famous reserves. Recent decades have seen increasing interest in the country's other national parks and protected areas, part of a conservation network that covers some 25 per cent of Tanzania's land area.

Deep in the heart of the country lie the Udzungwa Mountains, the most southerly – and largest – component in what is known to biologists as the Eastern Arc ecoregion. This crescent-shaped chain of geologically isolated upland areas, sometimes referred to as the "Galapagos of Africa" and regarded as one of the world's top biodiversity hotspots, extends from the Taita Hills in Kenya south and then westwards into the centre of Tanzania. Facing the prevailing moisture-laden winds from the Indian Ocean to the east, these disjunct highlands enjoy high levels of rainfall, their cool and markedly less seasonal climate very different from the generally hot and arid conditions of the surrounding lowlands. The fragmented and elevated nature of these "sky islands" has given rise to unique sets of flora and fauna, with very high levels of endemism. Each bloc supports species found nowhere else in the world.

RIGHT The scientific discovery of the Sanje Crested Mangabey in 1979 was the first in a series of remarkable encounters with new species in the Udzungwas. More are almost certain to come, as biologists continue to explore this remarkable area.

OPPOSITE The Udzungwas receive significantly higher rainfall than the lowland regions of Tanzania, a factor that is reflected in the lush vegetation and in the large number of rivers and waterfalls that dissect these uplands.

About one-fifth of the Udzungwas is protected by the Udzungwa Mountains National Park, which was established in 1992 and covers 1,990 square kilometres (770 square miles) of varied and often rugged terrain, rising to the highest peak, Lohomero, at 2,576 metres (8,450 feet). An extensive upland plateau supports traditional African mammals such as Lion *Panthera leo*, African Elephant *Loxodonta africana*, African Buffalo *Syncerus caffer* and Eland *Taurotragus oryx*, but more interesting in terms of wildlife are the extensive tracts of forest that cover the slopes. The vegetation here is extremely diverse, and although only 20 per cent or so of the park proper is closed-canopy forest, it includes a range of lowland and montane rainforest types. Indeed, it is probably the only place left in Africa where intact rainforest runs continuously from 300 metres (980 feet) or so above sea level up to over 2,000 metres (6,500 feet). In addition to their outstanding wildlife, the Udzungwas are home to some 700,000 people, who live largely by subsistence agriculture.

Although the British explorer John Hanning Speke gazed upon (and even painted) the Udzungwas in 1859, it is only in the last three decades or so that scientists have really studied them in earnest. Their research has revealed that the Udzungwas support the highest levels of biodiversity in all of Tanzania, with at least 18 endemic vertebrate species alongside a further 24 Eastern Arc endemic vertebrates and 36 Eastern Arc endemic or near-endemic trees. Over half of the plants found in the Udzungwas may be endemic to the wider region, and with many occurring only in these mountains. Particularly notable is the high incidence of species of *Saintpaulia* (African violets) and *Impatiens* ("Busy Lizzie"). With large areas of rainforest and other habitats still unexplored biologically, there is no doubt that further exciting discoveries remain to be made.

An early indication of how special this area is came in 1979, when a new species of monkey – the Sanje Crested Mangabey *Cercocebus sanje* – was observed here by scientists for the very first time. One

BELOW **The Udzungwa Red Colobus** has a distinctive spiky red crown and rufous hue to its otherwise dark tail. The name "colobus" is derived from the Greek word for "docked", a reference to the remnant thumb possessed by all members of this group of monkeys.

LEFT African Violets (genus *Saintpaulia*, with over 20 species described scientifically) are familiar houseplants in Europe and North America. In the wild, they favour the moist, shady conditions that are the hallmark of the Udzungwas and other uplands in the Eastern Arc.

BELOW Reptiles and amphibians show high rates of endemism in the Eastern Arc forests. Chameleons are proving to be a particularly interesting group; this is an undescribed species belonging to the *Kinyongia* genus.

of 12 primate species recorded in the Udzungwas so far, making these mountains one of the most important sites for this group in the entire African continent, the mangabey is found in just two separate populations some 100 kilometres (60 miles) apart and has an estimated total population in the range of 1,000–2,000 individuals. The other truly endemic Udzungwas primate, the Udzungwa Red Colobus *Piliocolobus gordonorum*, is more common but still highly restricted in range. In 2004 a near-endemic species, the Kipunji *Rungwecebus kipunji*, was found here in Ndundulu Forest. It had first been identified by biologists in the forests around Mount Rungwe in the south-west of Tanzania the previous year, and had proved to be not only a new species but a totally new genus.

New mammals continue to come to light in the Udzungwas. Among the most recent is the discovery of a previously unknown species of giant elephant-shrew, the Grey-faced Sengi *Rhynochocyon udzungwensis*. First caught on camera trap film in 2005, this extraordinary and ancient creature was then observed – and specimens trapped – the following year. At 700 grams (1.5 pounds), it is 25–50 per cent larger than any other known species of sengi, and is known from just two populations covering about 300 square kilometres (115 square miles) of forest in the Udzungwas.

Birdlife here is equally exciting, with several endemics and a whole range of regional specialities that are restricted to the Eastern Arc highlands. Of particular interest are the Rufous-winged Sunbird *Nectarinia rufipennis* and the Udzungwa Forest-partridge *Xenoperdix udzungwensis*, the latter first described scientifically in 1991 after the attention of two visiting ornithologists was

BELOW The Udzungwas contain several types of protected area under different categories of management. This view shows part of a catchment forest reserve known as the Udzungwa Scarp, which lies outside the national park but serves as an important wildlife corridor.

drawn to a strange pair of bird's feet in a local village cooking pot! Highly secretive, this is a relict species considered to be more closely related to partridges found in the foothills of the Himalayas than to any other African bird. Although initially understood to be restricted to the Udzungwas, in 2001 a second population was discovered in the Rubeho mountains, 150 kilometres (90 miles) to the north. However, these birds appear to be sufficiently distinct from those in the Udzungwas to qualify as a completely separate species.

The fact that such discoveries are still being made underlines how unique the Udzungwas are, and how highly insulated and unique the flora and fauna can be. Yet this dependence on what are often very small habitat niches also makes the wildlife potentially vulnerable, a predicament nowhere clearer than with the case of the Kihansi Spray Toad *Nectophrynoides asperginis*. Identified by scientists as recently as 1996, this tiny (only 19mm/0.75 inches long) mustard-coloured amphibian was found only in the spray zone around the Kihansi and Mhalala waterfalls in the southern Udzungwas. So specialized is it that it appears to have been restricted to an area only 2 hectares (5 acres) in extent, and has not been detected in seemingly identical conditions elsewhere in the area. Sadly, within months of its scientific discovery the toad was in trouble. The World Bank-funded construction of a dam designed to harness the power potential of the Kihansi River, a project that had begun before the toad was discovered, reduced the water flow by more than 80 per cent. The spray mist on which the toads depended was drastically reduced as a result, and the number of toads plummeted.

An artificial sprinkler system was installed to help recreate the required conditions but, with the majority of their habitat already changed irrevocably, the toads continued to disappear. The decision was therefore taken to establish a captive breeding programme, based at zoos in the United States. The dwindling numbers of wild toads then became infected by the chytrid fungus that is decimating amphibian populations elsewhere in the world. The fungus had not been known in Tanzania before and, ironically, may have been introduced to the Kihansi area via the boot of a visiting biologist working to conserve the toads. It proved to be the final straw; a 2004 site survey found no toads at all and the species was regarded as extinct in the wild. A reintroduction project involving captive-bred toads is now proposed, should the appropriate local habitat conditions be restored – a condition which may prove extremely difficult to realize.

The fate of the Kihansi Spray Toad serves to emphasize the fragility of the Udzungwa environment and underlines how vulnerable the whole associated ecosystem is to human activity. Continued habitat loss and fragmentation is a particular problem. The small-scale conversion of forest to farmland by

local people dates back many hundreds of years, but the process of forest clearance accelerated significantly during the colonial period, with the creation of extensive commercial tea and coffee estates, for example. Population pressure and associated demand for land continue to grow, processes that are accompanied by an increase in the exploitation of forest resources. This is especially the case in the less well-protected forest reserves outside the national park boundary, in some of which hunting for bushmeat appears to be commonplace, with the widespread use of firearms and the setting of traps and snares. Such activity, together with tree and pole cutting, is having a serious impact on the forest and on its mammals in particular. The situation is especially serious in the southern Udzungwa Scarp Forest, one of the largest and most important forests in the whole range.

On a wider level, the Udzungwas play a key role in maintaining ecological connectivity with other wildlife-rich ecosystems, notably the vast Selous Game Reserve to the south. Historically animals have moved into the Udzungwas in search of grazing during the dry season, doing so via habitat corridors that have permitted gene flow between different animal populations. In recent years these corridors have become increasingly subject to adverse change, and many traditional large mammal routes have already been blocked by the conversion of forest to farmland. This is especially so in the case of elephant movement between the Udzungwas and the Selous, with recent studies concluding that only one or two very narrow corridors might still be used. Wildlife populations are therefore becoming fragmented and vulnerable to extinction in ever-dwindling pockets of habitat. For this situation to be reversed, enhanced protection of the corridors and the forest reserves will need to be coupled with a system of community-based wildlife management areas that can ensure economic benefits to local people that are at least equal to those obtained from existing, often illegal, methods.

ABOVE **Amphibians abound in the cool, moist environment of the Udzungwas. Shown here is** *Hyperolius pictus*, **a montane species found across the highland areas of southern Tanzania and into adjacent Malawi and Zambia.**

ABOVE High levels of precipitation and mist ensure luxuriant canopy growth in the Udzungwa forests. The canopy is an ecosystem of its own, supporting complex niche communities of flora and fauna. Invertebrates are especially prolific here, and still little known scientifically.

RIGHT Restricted to the Udzungwas, the Red-snouted Wolf Snake *Lycophidion uzungwense* is nocturnal and feeds primarily on lizards and skinks. It can reach lengths of up to 60 centimetres (24 inches).

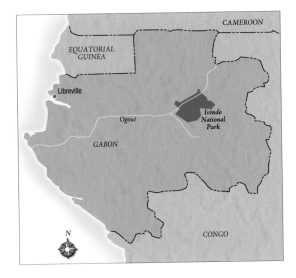

23. The Secret Forest Wildlife of Ivindo National Park, Gabon

In September 1999 American biologist and conservationist J. Michael Fay began a remarkable journey through central Africa. Travelling largely on foot, he spent 15 months on a 3,200-kilometre (2,000-mile) "Megatransect" expedition from the eastern part of the Democratic Republic of Congo westwards to Petit Louango on the coast of Gabon. His objective was to assess the ecological and environmental condition of the vast swathe of pristine rainforest, largely uninhabited by humans, that covers this part of the African continent and about which remarkably little was known. Fay suspected that this expanse of forest represented one of the last great wildlife regions of Africa, and almost certainly harboured important populations of animals. Yet little could he – or anyone else – have anticipated the scale of what he was to find there, or the implications of these discoveries.

As a result of Fay's findings, in 2002 the Gabonese government under President Omar Bongo declared a network of 13 national parks across the country, amounting to 28,500 square kilometres (11,000 square miles) in total – 11 per cent of its land area. The new parks included several of the wildlife-rich areas through which Fay had travelled, one of which was Ivindo, 3,000 square kilometres (1,160 square miles) of mainly pristine lowland rainforest between the Ivindo and Ogooué rivers and straddling the Equator. The park contains some of central Africa's most spectacular waterfalls, but is perhaps best known for the remarkable wildlife concentrations that Fay discovered around Langoué Bai, a 20-hectare (50-acre) clearing in the heart of the rainforest.

The discovery of such clearings, known by the local name of *bais*, was one of the more astonishing outcomes of Fay's journey through the forests of the Congo Basin. The received wisdom hitherto was that the rainforest simply rolled on, uninterrupted, for thousands of kilometres, except where disrupted by the activities of man, notably by logging and agriculture. The concept of there being natural clearings on such a scale had never been given serious consideration. Furthermore,

OPPOSITE TOP AND BOTTOM **Langoué Bai is a magnificent setting for wildlife observation. Groups of elephants (top) emerge from the backdrop of primary rainforest to drink, bathe and take up minerals, while families of gorillas sit out in the open (bottom), feeding and resting. Here a superb silverback male stands surrounded by his females and offspring.**

BELOW **The Mingouli Falls on the Ivindo River, a tributary of the Ogooué. As with most areas of lowland rainforest, rainfall levels are high here throughout much of the year and the rivers and waterfalls in the park are particularly impressive.**

OPPOSITE TOP **Totally at home in swamps and marshes, the Sitatunga is a good swimmer and assisted in these watery environments by its long, splayed hooves. These enable it to walk over aquatic vegetation without sinking. It will dive underwater when frightened, becoming almost completely submerged and with only its nose showing above water.**

the concentration at Langoué Bai of large numbers of traditionally elusive large mammals was nothing short of a revelation. For here, grazing and drinking peacefully out in the open, away from the dark recesses of the forest itself, were herds of normally secretive Forest Elephant *Loxodonta cyclotis* and Forest Buffalo *Syncerus caffer nanus*, alongside antelope species such as Bongo *Tragelaphus eurycerus* and Sitatunga *Tragelaphus spekii*, and – perhaps most remarkable of all – families of Western Lowland Gorilla *Gorilla gorilla*, calmly sitting around relaxing and feeding. As a result, Ivindo – together with Gabon's other national parks – has become one of the most exciting and unusual wildlife-watching destinations in the world.

More than 1,000 individual Forest Elephants have been recorded visiting Langoué Bai. Now accepted by most authorities as a species distinct from the "other" African elephant *Loxodonta africana*, these elephants exhibit subtle but important differences from their larger cousins. They have five toes on their forefoot and four on the hindfoot (compared to four and three respectively, in the case of *africana*), more rounded ears and straighter, downward-pointing tusks. The latter are doubtless an evolutionary response to life in dense forest, in which tusks that pointed upwards would be an impediment to ease of movement through the thick undergrowth. Forest Elephants are also smaller in size, a male attaining an average shoulder height of 2.2 metres (7 feet 2 inches) compared to 3.3 metres (10 feet 10 inches) in the case of *africana*. The different habitat preferences are also significant; it is highly unusual to see Forest Elephants as easily as at Langoué, as they are generally restricted to dense tracts of forest from which they hardly ever emerge.

The opportunity to observe Forest Elephants out in the open is contributing hugely to scientific understanding of their ecology. In most other localities these are highly secretive animals, about which little is understood. What has become clear, however, is that poaching is taking its toll of central Africa's "secret" elephants. Discoveries of stashes of illegal ivory, the finding of carcases and traumatized young elephants, and reports of nocturnal hunts by poaching gangs all indicate a population under increasing pressure. Although some big "tuskers" visit the *bai*, elsewhere in Gabon they are an increasingly rare sight, already killed by poachers for their ivory. Reliable figures of exactly how many Forest Elephants survive in total are virtually impossible to establish, but it is almost certain that their numbers are in decline across much of their Central and West African range.

Even in the relatively secure environment of Langoué there is a marked difference between the behaviour shown towards humans by the elephants and the attitude of the gorillas that also

BELOW **Encounters at the waterhole provide an opportunity for young male elephants to test their strength and establish their dominance (or otherwise) over their peers. Sadly, mature males – "big tuskers" – are few and far between in Ivindo, having already been poached for their ivory.**

OPPOSITE BOTTOM **The distinctive white facial markings and body stripes of the shy and reclusive Bongo serve as perfect camouflage in its typical habitat of dense forest, helping to break up its outline in the dappled light. Yet at Langoué Bai groups of Bongo graze out in the open, behaviour almost unknown anywhere else.**

frequent the open grassland and swamps of the *bai*. Watching gorillas interact with one another is one of the great wildlife experiences and made all the more special at Langoué by the fact that many of the gorillas here are unfamiliar with humans. Showing little or no fear, and considerable curiosity, they are generally unfazed by human presence. The elephants, on the other hand, are very wary and suspicious, and always unpredictable. This is almost certainly because most of them range widely through the forest in search of food and most, if not all, of the park's elephant population is likely to have come into contact with humans at some point – often with negative consequences for the elephants. As a result, they have learned to mistrust humans. The gorillas, however, move around within a much smaller home range of often only a few square kilometres and many will never have encountered *homo sapiens*.

Despite the trusting nature of the so-called "naïve" gorillas, considerable effort is made at Langoué to avoid excessive interaction between human visitors – who watch the activity from discreetly located raised platforms at the side of the *bai* – and the wildlife that gathers here. Sensitive management of the growing number of people wishing to see this extraordinary spectacle is essential to ensure that the animals continue to visit and behave in as natural a manner as when Michael Fay first discovered the site. Most of the animals are drawn to the *bai* owing to the availability of food – the gorillas are especially attracted by the abundance of aquatic plants, for example – and by the presence in the soil of various minerals. These are a particular lure to elephants, and it is likely that the character and size of the *bai* itself have been shaped by decades, if not centuries, of elephant digging activity. These immense animals will often kneel down and excavate the soil with their tusks, to reach the minerals below. They also come to the *bai* to bathe and drink, frequently in herds of 30 or more.

LEFT This aerial view of Langoué Bai shows clearly the dramatic change in landscape it represents, when seen in the context of the vast expanse of rainforest. Similar natural clearings have been discovered elsewhere in the Congo Basin, but few are as rich in wildlife as here in Ivindo.

RIGHT A family group of elephants arrives at the *bai*. As elephants need to drink every day, visits take on something of a regular routine, with baby elephants carefully escorted by their mother and other female members of the group.

Individual gorillas and elephants are recorded by scientists working from the research camp based near the *bai*, with the distinguishing features of each animal noted in sketches or by photographs. A few elephants have been fitted with GPS transmitters, so that their movements through the forest can be tracked more effectively. A more meaningful picture is now emerging of how these animals use the forest, and how large an area they cover in their search for food and water. The gorillas are a source of particular interest, as elsewhere in Central Africa they are facing a range of potentially disastrous threats. Foremost among these is the demand for bushmeat (see below), but habitat loss is also a concern, as is the spread of the Ebola virus. Since 2002 Ebola has been responsible for the deaths of hundreds of gorillas and chimpanzees (as well as smaller numbers of humans) on the northern edges of Gabon and the Democratic Republic of Congo, reducing the ape population in some places by over 50 per cent.

Langoué provides a fascinating window on the hitherto hidden lives of large forest-dwelling mammals. The lack of a recent tradition of human settlement within Ivindo has kept the local wildlife largely safe from, and unaffected by, hunting and disturbance. However, pressures are now building from outside. Large areas of forest adjacent to the park boundaries are slated for logging, and the related access roads – some already under construction – will make the park's pristine and wildlife-rich forests more accessible to hunters and illegal loggers. There is also a massive bushmeat industry in Gabon, with the markets of the provincial towns and villages, as well as the capital city, Libreville, full of butchered wildlife on sale, including gorilla and elephant parts. Visitors en route to Ivindo are often confronted with the sight of dead monkeys and duikers hanging for sale outside houses and roadside stalls. With the more accessible forests of Gabon already largely stripped of their larger birds and animals, hunters are now turning their attention to those harboured by the protected areas. Conservation groups such as the Wildlife Conservation Society and World Wide Fund for Nature are working to contain the problem and to develop sustainable ecotourism as an alternative means of economic livelihood for rural populations.

BELOW Mature male Western Lowland Gorillas have a distinctive rufous forehead and crown. This individual also has the distinctive silver back, characteristic of a male in his prime. These are supremely powerful animals, capable of causing serious injury to each other and to potential attackers.

OPPOSITE Baby gorillas usually weigh just under 2 kilograms (4.4 pounds) at birth and, like the offspring of *homo sapiens*, are totally helpless. They begin to crawl at about nine weeks or so, and by nine months are able to walk. Mother gorillas are highly attentive at all times.

24. The Indris of the Madagascar Rainforest

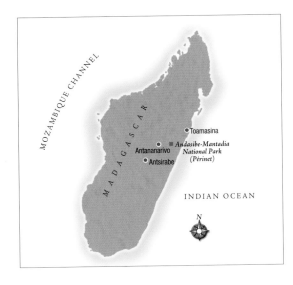

One of the most evocative wildlife experiences anywhere in the world can be enjoyed at dawn in the rainforest of the Andasibe–Mantadia (Périnet) National Park in Madagascar. At first light, from amid the tree canopy that arches overhead, comes the bizarre "song" of the Indri, one of the most sacred animals to the local Malagasy people. A sequence of eerie trumpeting wails, each rising to a higher-pitched "wwwhip" towards the end, these calls signal the presence initially of one animal, and then of several more as others join in this unique dawn chorus. Indri singing is usually sequential, in the sense that different groups will call repeatedly in response to one another, signalling their territorial claims over particular areas of the forest. The resulting cacophony can travel up to 3 kilometres (over 1.5 miles) and, once heard, is never forgotten.

The Indri or Babakoto *Indri indri* is the largest species of lemur and one of the most distinctive. With a body length of up to 70 centimetres (28 inches) and weighing as much as 10 kilograms (20 pounds) or more, its black-and-white coat, engaging "teddy-bear" ears and insignificant tail (the shortest of any lemur species) make identification easy. Indris live in small family groups, usually of between two and five animals, and are almost exclusively arboreal – it is very unusual to see them down on the ground. They are also among the most diurnal of all lemurs and, with a slow metabolism, are generally sluggish in the early morning. Their day invariably gets off to a slow start, and Indris are often to be seen sitting around in trees in the morning sun in an effort to "get going". When sufficiently galvanized by the warmth, they will start to forage for food.

OPPOSITE Indris are quite unmistakable. One of the best times to observe them is in the early morning, when they are often seen lounging about in the sun "waking up" before they start to move through the trees in search of food.

LEFT Much of the Andasibe–Mantadia Park is dissected by mountain streams, along which there are many excellent habitat niches for a wide range of reptiles and amphibians. Ferns and palms are typical vegetation in such situations.

Once active, Indris can be spectacular jumpers, capable of spanning as much 5 metres (16.5 feet) in a single leap. They often string together a dramatic sequence of such jumps as they move through the forest from tree to tree in search of things to eat, usually propelling themselves from trunk to trunk using their long and powerful back legs. They live mostly on leaves, and have been recorded feeding on over 70 different species of plant. They pick through foliage delicately, selecting choice morsels with their mouth and feeding quite deliberately and rather slowly in a decidedly more lethargic manner than most other species of lemur.

Relationships between male and female Indris are equally sedate. The species is monogamous, and mating takes place each year in January or February, after little in the way of extravagant courtship. The single baby is born four months later, and for the first few months of its life clings to its mother's underbelly before transferring to her back once it has gained confidence. Indri babies are often very playful, tumbling about the trees (and over their parents) with the exuberant abandon that makes primates so engaging to watch.

The best place to see Indris is the Analamazaotra/Périnet Reserve, which is close to the town of Andasibe, and which was amalgamated with the Mantadia National Park to create the larger park. The reserve covers a little over 800 hectares (1,970 acres) and, despite the logging of most of its larger trees during the twentieth century, it remains an important area of mid-altitude montane rainforest, albeit physically isolated from other areas of forest by farmland and plantations. Several groups of the resident Indris here have been habituated to human presence and it would be an unlucky visitor indeed that did not see, or at least hear, them. It is not such an easy proposition to catch up with the several other lemur species that are present here, as their numbers are small and they are perhaps best looked for in the Mantadia section of the park, which at 10,000 hectares

ABOVE **Although generally rather languid in their movements, Indris will sometimes have sudden bursts of energy. At such times they will jump about from tree to tree, covering considerable distances in just a few leaps and moving quickly from one group of trees to another.**

OPPOSITE **The Périnet reserve is densely forested, with a great diversity of plants and trees and a generally thick understorey. This can make human access difficult, a factor that has helped ensure that the wildlife here is largely undisturbed.**

OPPOSITE The Diademed Sifaka is regarded as "critically endangered", largely as a result of habitat loss. Hunting is less of a concern, as for many Malagasy people the killing of lemurs is regarded as taboo and they are usually unmolested.

(24,700 acres) is much more extensive (and also more varied in terms of altitude). The vegetation is broadly similar to that in the reserve, with a dense understorey including stands of bamboo and many tree ferns (*Cyathea* spp.) and an overhead canopy composed of species of *Dalbergia, Ravensara, Tambourissa, Vernonia* and *Weinmannia*. Orchids and epiphytes are common.

In Mantadia it is possible to see groups of Diademed Sifaka *Propithecus diadema*, generally a rather elusive lemur but one that can, with patience and luck, be seen well here. It is the largest sifaka and arguably the most attractive. Although other species of sifaka will descend to the ground quite readily and even the adults can be seen engaged in playful behaviour, with high-spirited bouts of chasing and what appear to be games of "tag", the Diademed resembles the Indri in much of its behaviour and is overwhelmingly arboreal, with a similar "cling-and-leap" form of locomotion. It is, however, generally more mobile than the Indri, and groups can travel up to 2 kilometres (1.25 miles) daily when foraging for food. They are primarily folivorous, but will also eat fruit, seeds and bark. Each group (usually numbering between two and 10 individuals) maintains a home territory of typically 20–30 hectares (50–75 acres), which is vigorously defended against other groups of the same species.

Sifakas have very few natural enemies. Foremost among these is the extraordinary Fossa *Cryptoprocta ferox*. Looking rather like a cross between a dog and a cat, the Fossa is the largest carnivore on Madagascar and can reach up to 2 metres (6.5 feet) in length, half of which is tail. It is as much at home in the tree canopy as on the ground and mostly hunts by night and at dawn, a time when lemurs are either asleep or at their most inactive. The sudden appearance of the highly agile and aggressive Fossa in their midst is guaranteed to provoke an outburst of frantic lemur alarm calls. Fossas are thinly distributed and nowhere common, however, and with a total population estimated at fewer than 2,500 are considered endangered.

Andasibe–Mantadia is outstanding for amphibians and reptiles, with around 100 species of frog recorded here and several species of chameleon present, the latter often readily found along the tracks and roadsides. Madagascar is home to a remarkable total of 70 or so species of chameleon, comprising half of the world's total number, and most of them are endemic. Among those found in the park are Parson's Chameleon *Calumma parsonii*, the world's largest species and capable of exceeding 60 centimetres (2 feet) in length, and Nose-horned Chameleon *C. nasutus*, the smallest representative of the genus. Madagascar's chameleons are under threat from both habitat destruction and illegal collection for the pet trade, with local extinctions already sadly commonplace in some parts of the island. One of the most noteworthy reptiles found in the park is the Madagascar Tree Boa *Sanzinia madagascariensis*, a variably coloured species of snake which, although primarily arboreal, is regularly found at ground level, where its cryptic patterning provides excellent camouflage among the leaf litter. It preys mainly on small mammals and birds and can attain a length of up to 2.5 metres (8 feet 2 inches).

Birdlife in Mantadia is impressive and includes a number of iconic species at or near the top of any birdwatcher's wishlist. These include four species of ground roller: Pitta-like *Atelornis pittoides*, Rufous-headed *A. crossleyi*, Scaly *Brachyteracias squamiger* and Short-legged *B. leptosomus*, none of which is easy to see. All live on or near the forest floor, usually frequenting the shadiest corners where they forage for worms, larvae and other invertebrates. The ecology and behaviour of ground rollers are imperfectly understood and it is possible that some species are not as rare as previously believed; their furtive habits simply make them virtually impossible to study closely.

Madagascar has already lost as much as 90 per cent of its native forest cover and the continued fragmentation of what remains is an urgent environmental and conservation problem. The creation of Andasibe–Mantadia National Park was in part an attempt to boost the viability of the Analamazaotra/Périnet Reserve, which was proving too small to ensure the genetic viability of the wildlife populations it was ostensibly protecting, notably the Indris. Surrounded by farmland and degraded secondary forest, it is impossible for animals to expand into new areas of suitable habitat. The restoration of physical connections between the two ecosystems is therefore of paramount importance, and work is under way to plant linked clusters of native trees so that a corridor of habitat can be established between the two main areas of the park.

BELOW **Ground rollers (below left, Scaly, below right, Pitta-like) are spectacular birds but very difficult to see well. However, local bird guides are highly skilled at finding these elusive species and can usually be relied upon to track them down, even in the densest of undergrowth.**

ABOVE The male Parson's Chameleon has two warty horns on its nose, and will head-butt other males in fights to establish dominance and access to females. Mating only every other year, the females incubate their eggs for 18 months or even longer.

RIGHT Madagascar continues to lose yet more of its rainforest every year. Population pressure and grinding levels of poverty are the main reasons why forest is cleared to make way for subsistence crops, but ecotourism and wildlife-interest holidays are making a difference in certain locations.

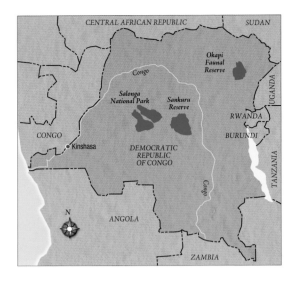

25. The Bonobos and Okapis of the Congo Rainforest

The Congo Basin supports one of the largest tracts of tropical rainforest in the world, second only to that found in the Amazon Basin. Extending over almost 4 million square kilometres (1.5 million square miles) and bisected by the mighty 4,700-kilometre (2,900-mile) long River Congo, this forest makes up 70 per cent of Africa's entire plant cover and supports exceptionally high levels of biodiversity. Over 10,000 different animal species are known to live here, with more undoubtedly awaiting scientific discovery. Many parts of the forest remain scarcely better known to the outside world today than in the 1870s, when Western explorers such as Henry Morton Stanley made their first journeys across the region. In recent decades political instability and almost constant civil strife and warfare have rendered some of the more ecologically interesting areas inaccessible to researchers, as well as disrupting and dispersing many of the local human inhabitants.

Over half of the Congo Basin rainforest lies within the Democratic Republic of Congo (DRC), where scientists are discovering an increasing number of biodiversity hotspots, in part a result

OPPOSITE **Adult Bonobos are often hunted for food and their young taken for the illegal pet trade. Rescuing these young animals and subsequently caring for them in sanctuaries are among the current conservation initiatives for this increasingly endangered species.**

RIGHT The rainforests of the Congo Basin are vast, and still largely unexplored by scientists. Political upheaval and security concerns have made consistent research here problematic, but the biodiversity of the region is not in doubt and rightly continues to attract the interest of conservationists.

of these forests being among the few African examples to have survived the last ice age, 10,000 years ago. The high local rates of endemism extend across almost all floral and faunal groups, and include large forest-dwelling mammal species that remained unknown to science until the twentieth century. Foremost among these are the Bonobo *Pan paniscus* and the Okapi *Okapia johnstoni*, both of which are endemic to the DRC and are now the subject of particular conservation interest.

It is believed that Bonobos – formerly known as Dwarf or Pygmy Chimpanzees – split from the Common Chimpanzee *Pan troglodytes* about one million years ago, after ancestral chimpanzees had dispersed over a wide area as regional climatic and habitat conditions improved. Some groups later became cut off from the main population as a result of changing landscape features, such as expanding rivers, and subsequently evolved in isolation. The first scientific descriptions of the species were only made in the 1920s, since when research has revealed that with a DNA 98 percent in common with *Homo sapiens*, Bonobos are one of our nearest relatives. Evidence suggests that they are more closely related to humans than to gorillas, and particular attention has focused on the differences between Bonobos and Common Chimpanzees as a way of understanding early hominid history.

Whilst the two species are broadly similar in terms of diet and general ecology, there are several key differences. The most immediately obvious involves habitat – Bonobos are exclusively rainforest inhabitants, whereas Common Chimps will range over a wider variety of terrain. Physically, Bonobos are more slender in frame than Chimps, with longer limbs and less developed chests, and when adult their faces are black rather than flesh-coloured. However, it is the nature of their interaction with their own kind which perhaps most notably stands them apart from Chimps. Bonobos are decidedly less aggressive and antagonistic, and usually eschew confrontation, whether that be from within their family group or with unfamiliar Bonobos with which they come into contact. In particular, much interest has centred on the high incidence among Bonobos of sexual behaviour, which is used in a variety of situations unrelated to reproduction, such as greeting, conflict resolution and reconciliation, and takes place readily between individuals of the same sex as well as between male and female.

OPPOSITE **Looking like an animal made up of parts from other species, the elusive Okapi is superbly adapted to life in the rainforest environment. Photographing wild Okapis is exceedingly difficult and usually only possible through the use of camera traps, as here.**

LEFT **Despite their close physical resemblance to Common Chimpanzees, Bonobos are very different animals. Their female-dominated society is much more peaceful and harmonious than the male-dominated social structure of Chimps, and infanticide and lethal forms of aggression are unknown.**

Bonobos occur only in the central Congo Basin and one of the largest populations is found in Salonga National Park, established in 1970 and declared a World Heritage Site in 1984. Africa's largest protected rainforest area, it covers some 36,500 square kilometres (14,100 square miles), in two blocks that are separated by a 40–45-kilometre (25–28-mile) wide corridor. The park extends over a series of river valleys and includes various types of mostly pristine forest, from seasonally inundated swamp and riverine evergreen through to dry semi-deciduous, the latter found on the higher ground between the valleys. There are also areas of savannah/forest mosaic habitats, which are high in biodiversity. The evergreen forests are dominated by *Gilbertiodendron dewevrei* alongside *G. ogoouense* and *Brachystegia laurentii*, with flood-tolerant species such as *Oubanguia africana*, *Scytopetalum pierrianum* and *Guibourtia demeusei* more prevalent in wetter areas. Much of the park remains unexplored.

Although research is ongoing and the true picture of Salonga's biodiversity remains unclear, the indications are that the park supports substantial populations of almost all of the classic Congo Basin wildlife species. These include Forest Elephant *Loxodonta cyclotis*, Forest Buffalo *Syncerus caffer nanus*, Leopard *Panthera pardus*, Red River Hog *Potamochoerus porcus ubangensis*, three species of duiker (*Cephalophus* spp.), Sitatunga *Tragelaphus spekii*, Bushbuck *T. scriptus*, and Bongo *T. euryceros*. A wide variety of less well-known species also occurs, such as Water Chevrotain *Hyemoschus aquaticus*, Giant Pangolin *Manis gigantea* and Aquatic or Fishing Genet *Genetta piscivora*, as well as a particularly interesting variety of primates. As well as the Bonobo, these include four other Congo endemics, Black Mangabey *Lophocebus aterrimus*, Golden-bellied Mangabey *Cercocebus galeritus chrysogaster*, Salonga Guenon or Dryas Monkey *Cercopithecus dryas* and Thollon's Red Colobus, *Piliocolobus tholloni*.

Away from the central Congo Basin, one of Africa's more extraordinary species has only been known to science for little over a century. Descended from a variety of giraffe-like species that once roamed the wet savannahs of much of the continent, the enigmatic Okapi is placed in its own genus. During the nineteenth century European explorers and sportsmen were intrigued by the rumours of a 'forest zebra' that lived deep in the forests of the eastern Congo and was known only to the local inhabitants, the Mbuti and Efe Pygmies, who hunted it for meat. Skins showing the striped pattern of the Okapi's hindquarters only served to reinforce the idea among outsiders that this was a type of zebra. Only with further discoveries made by a 1901 expedition, which first found tracks – showing the animal was cloven-hoofed and therefore not a type of horse – and then obtained a specimen, was the true identity of this almost mythical beast properly established.

OPPOSITE **The African or Two-spotted Palm Civet** *Nandinia binotata* **is arboreal and an excellent climber, often living high in the rainforest canopy. Omnivorous in diet, it preys on lizards, insects, small birds and eggs, as well as being partial to fruit and even carrion.**

LEFT **Perfectly camouflaged for life among the leaves of the forest floor, the Gaboon Viper** *Bitis gabonica* **is highly venomous and has some of the longest fangs of any snake. However, like most snakes it is not aggressive and poses little threat to humans if left alone.**

ABOVE The Ituri Forest is home to two Pygmy groups, the Efe and Mbuti. Both follow a semi-nomadic, hunter-gatherer lifestyle, living off game (which they shoot with arrows), fish, fungi, fruit and other forest products. Their knowledge of the forest is encyclopaedic and still largely untapped by outsiders.

Until recently (see below), Okapis were believed to be restricted to the rainforests of the eastern DRC, most notably the Ituri Forest, where the Okapi Faunal Reserve is located. Declared a World Heritage Site in 1996, the reserve covers 13,750 square kilometres (5,300 square miles) – about 20 per cent of the Ituri Forest – and is home to a range of wildlife similar to that found in Salonga National Park, with the exception of the Bonobo. Birdlife is particularly rich here, with over 350 species recorded and the reserve being regarded as one of the top forest sites for birds in all of Africa. In addition to protecting approximately 5,000 wild Okapis (out of a total world population of perhaps 30,000), the reserve also includes a research centre. This was initially established in the 1950s as a means of supplying Okapis to zoos worldwide, but has since concentrated on ensuring that the future of the species is made more secure through captive breeding programmes and research into wild Okapi ecology.

Like giraffes, Okapis are browsers, gathering leaves, buds and fruit from trees by means of their long, extendable tongue. They often feed off shrubs in areas of dense forest, especially along small rivers and streams or on the edge of clearings, where light can filter through to encourage the new growth they require. Their cryptic hide markings serve them well in the dappled shade of this environment. Highly secretive animals, they are solitary in nature, only seeking the company of other Okapis when interested in mating. Whilst their numbers are thought to be stable, the poaching of animals for their meat is a growing problem, as it is for Bonobos, which are also in demand from the illegal pet trade.

Bonobo and Okapi conservation received a potentially major boost in 2006 with the establishment of the Sankuru Nature Reserve, a 30,570-square-kilometre- (11,800-square-mile) tract of primary rainforest to the east of Salonga National Park and in the very heart of the DRC. Home to important numbers of Bonobos (as well as other primates and herds of Forest Elephant), Sankuru has also been revealed to support a population of Okapi, hitherto known only from the north-east of the country. This remarkable discovery underlines how scientific knowledge of

ABOVE Hunting for bushmeat
is rife across much of West and
Central Africa, including the
Congo. Here a vendor displays his
menu of species, a macabre list
that includes monkey, pangolin,
porcupine, tortoise and *chat-tigre*,
the latter a probable reference
to Serval *Leptailurus serval*.

much of this region is still in its infancy, and how important it is for biological survey-work to be undertaken before decisions are taken on the potential exploitation of this remarkable resource.

Although the Congo was the first African country to establish a national park (in 1925, in the Virunga mountains, to protect Mountain Gorillas *Gorilla beringei beringei*), in recent decades the DRC has become trapped in a downward spiral of mismanagement and war. The virtual collapse of civil society and a perilous security situation have made accurate wildlife surveys and conservation management all but impossible, and even within protected areas such as Salonga National Park, the hunting of wildlife, often with automatic weapons, is widespread. Trafficking in bushmeat is rife, and the prospect of commercial logging potentially threatens much of the rainforest, of which some 60 per cent is estimated to be loggable.

However, with various peace deals now in place there are grounds for cautious optimism. The current DRC government is committed to increasing the amount of the country covered by protected areas to 15 per cent (from the current figure of 10 per cent) and conservation organizations, both local and international, are working towards the rehabilitation of the country's once impressive national park network. Absolutely central to the future conservation of the wildlife will be the enforcement of the rule of law within the parks and protected areas, alongside the development of economic alternatives to the bushmeat trade and illegal logging activity. For many Congolese, the forest has traditionally supplied all their needs, but in an increasing number of areas the levels of exploitation are currently running well ahead of that which is sustainable. As a consequence this could lead to the destruction of the very resource on which people depend.

Rainforests Today: Now and the Future

The rapidly diminishing extent of the world's rainforests, so often the focus of high-profile media coverage and even the periodic attention of Hollywood celebrities, needs little by way of introduction. So many figures on the alarming rate of loss have been bandied around that to repeat them here would be meaningless. Suffice to say that we are currently cutting down rainforests at well over twice the rate of fifty years ago and that if this level of destruction continues we shall see the disappearance of virtually all the planet's rainforests – and of the wildlife they sustain – within another half a century or so.

The implications of such a loss are, of course, immense. Climate change would inevitably accelerate and rainfall levels worldwide are likely to drop considerably, with potentially disastrous consequences for agriculture. Global biodiversity levels would be damaged irreparably, with many thousands – probably millions – of rainforest-dependent species wiped out. Once the forest and its products have gone, millions of people would find themselves living on marginal land incapable of sustaining them in the long term, and so would be forced to relocate. The destruction of the rainforests could in fact result in a massive food crisis and large-scale human migration, with catastrophic political and social upheaval.

Rainforests are subject to many different types of exploitation, with global, national and local priorities for rainforest management (including its removal) frequently linked to the market prices of particular commodities. These can be products from the rainforest itself – timber, primarily – or crops that compete with the rainforest for land and are therefore potential replacements for it. Rates of deforestation are therefore often market-dependent, slowing when certain prices fall and accelerating when they rise. For example, the growth in palm oil prices through the 1980s and '90s resulted in the clearance of many millions of hectares of rainforest across Southeast Asia and its replacement by oil-palm plantations. Robust beef prices had the same effect in the south-east

BELOW **Over 1 billion people now live in the rainforest belt. For many of the forest's original inhabitants the pressure to give up their traditional lifestyle and exploit the forest in new ways can be both overwhelming and bewildering. Here, in a telling juxtaposition, a Sakai hunter sits by logged timber at Riau on Sumatra.**

OPPOSITE **Historically, temperate rainforests have been at just as much risk of logging as their tropical counterparts. Vast tracts have been destroyed in North America, for example, with protected areas such as the Quinault Forest in the Olympic National Park (shown here) a reminder of what has been lost.**

Amazon Basin's so-called "arc of fire" during the same period, when cattle ranching expanded hugely. More recently, the commercial farming of prawns destined for European and North American supermarkets has prompted the destruction of many thousands of square kilometres of mangrove forest. And, in a grimly ironic twist, the developed world's dash for biofuels to help reduce carbon dioxide emissions has perversely helped increase pressure to clear tropical rainforest and plant the land with the requisite source crops.

Spurred on by high global demand for timber and paper, logging remains the single biggest source of rainforest destruction. Much of this activity is illicit, with at least 70 per cent of the timber harvest in certain countries composed of illegally felled trees. In many cases, the relevant authorities turn a blind eye or fail to enforce legislation. For local people the short-term economic rewards from such activity can often be far in excess of what they can expect to earn via other means, and so they are usually willing participants in the process. In some rainforests illegal logging and the hunting of forest animals for bushmeat are the mainstays of the local economy and the largest sources of employment.

In this respect, one of the greatest enemies of the rainforest is poverty. For many people, trying to live on or even below basic subsistence levels, the forest is understandably viewed as a resource to be plundered immediately, regardless of longer-term implications. In February 2008, for example, violent rioting broke out in a remote part of northern Brazil in defence of illegal local loggers who were threatened by government officials with arrest and the seizure of their timber. The people who objected so vehemently to the attempted action by the authorities were not wealthy landowners or businessmen seeking to protect their investment portfolio. They were mostly poverty-stricken villagers, for whom the illegal felling of forest trees was their only source of income and livelihood.

Yet evidence suggests that rainforests can have more economic value if they are retained and their products harvested on a sustainable basis through agro-forestry, rather than sacrificed for a quick return. In this respect education is key, but there is little time left to inform and persuade. Rapidly rising population levels – at their highest in the developing countries that harbour most of the surviving rainforests – mean that the pressure on potentially cultivable land is already overwhelming in places. Subsistence farming, based on traditional slash-and-burn techniques,

BELOW The opportunity of observing large mammals such as elephants and gorillas in close promixity to one another, as here in Odzala National Park in Congo is something overseas tourists are prepared to pay handsomely for. In this sense rainforests can pay their way as natural habitats rather than as stores of timber.

ABOVE LEFT Education is key to encouraging local people to value wildlife more highly alive than dead, as here with this poster in Vietnam. More important, however, is the creation of sustainable economic alternatives to the pattern of hunting, trapping and exploitation.

ABOVE RIGHT The sensitive development of ecotourism can help local communities if structured appropriately. The Napo Wildlife Centre in Amazonian Ecuador is owned and run by the local Añangu people, many of whom work at the lodge and as wildlife guides. All revenues from the Centre go to the local community.

traditionally had little overall impact on large tracts of rainforest when human population density was light. But it is a very different proposition when many thousands of often landless squatters move into a forest area from what are frequently already devastated landscapes elsewhere and proceed to clear, burn and cultivate the land.

Ironically, the very people who can help instruct the rest of us in how to live sustainably from the rainforest are those who have lost out most in the undignified scramble to plunder this precious environment. Indigenous rainforest people are disappearing as fast as the trees around them. Increasingly "absorbed" into mainstream society or forced to abandon their traditional way of life simply because their forest has become fragmented or, in some cases, been sold over their heads, these people hold the key to the real value of the rainforest. It is already established, for example, that a majority of the plants known to be useful in cancer treatment are found only in rainforest habitats. Yet as only a small percentage of rainforest plants have been analyzed scientifically in terms of their medical properties, we have but the scantiest understanding of the full potential contribution that rainforests could make to pharmaceutical science.

Saving rainforests is therefore directly related to saving ourselves. International conservation organizations such as the World Land Trust, World Wide Fund for Nature, Wildlife Conservation Society, Rainforest Foundation and The Nature Conservancy work with local partners to protect rainforest through a range of strategies, including land acquisition and the establishment of sustainable, community-run reserves. The most successful projects focus on alleviating poverty and creating the mechanisms by which the rainforest is worth more to local people as a living entity than as a stack of timber and a field of crops. This can be achieved locally in many ways, from ecotourism to tree-planting funded by the selling of carbon offsets. Yet at the same time pressure is mounting within poorer countries especially to land the biggest rainforest prize of all: the wealth represented by the vast mineral and oil reserves sitting beneath their rainforests. Too tempting a bounty to ignore, such riches come with a high environmental price. Existing mining activity in parts of the Amazon, for example, reveals all too graphically the devastating pollution and environmental degradation that can result from mining and oil extraction in rainforests. This dilemma requires international rather than purely local resolutions, and undoubtedly a role for the world's richer nations in compensating financially those countries that choose to protect their forests rather than destroy them. One thing is certain, however – the future of the world's rainforests, and the solutions required to save them, will be as complex as the extraordinary ecosystems they support.

Site Gazetteer

AUSTRALIA	Site 8 (page 80)
BANGLADESH	Site 6 (page 64)
BORNEO (MALAYSIA)	Site 2 (page 30)
BRAZIL	Site 15 (page 146)
CANADA	Site 12 (page 116)
CHILE	Site 18 (page 170)
DEM. REP. CONGO	Site 25 (page 230)
ECUADOR	Sites 13 and 14 (pages 128 and 138)
GABON	Site 23 (page 214)
GHANA	Site 21 (page 198)
GUYANA	Site 16 (page 156)
INDIA	Sites 1 and 6 (pages 20 and 64)
MADAGASCAR	Site 24 (page 222)
NEW ZEALAND	Site 9 (page 90)
PANAMA	Site 19 (page 178)
PAPUA NEW GUINEA	Site 10 (page 98)
PHILIPPINES	Site 3 (page 40)
SUMATRA (INDONESIA)	Site 5 (page 56)
TANZANIA	Site 22 (page 206)
THAILAND	Site 7 (page 72)
UGANDA	Site 20 (page 188)
USA	Site 11 (page 108)
VIETNAM	Site 4 (page 48)
WEST INDIES	Site 17 (page 164)

Resources

There is a wealth of travel companies, both specialist and otherwise, operating tours to the rainforests covered in this book. It is worth looking carefully at the detail of itineraries and the amount of time spent in the field, as well as to what extent – if indeed, at all – the company concerned is making efforts to contribute to the conservation of the places to which it runs tours. Reading previous tour reports and dossiers is a critical element of pre-trip research, as is a basic degree of familiarisation with an area's flora and fauna via the vast amount of material now available both on the printed page and through the internet. Some rainforests can also be visited easily by independent travellers, although in such cases is always worth employing the services of a local guide. This not only helps reinforce the economic value of the forest and its wildlife on a direct level to those that matter most, but should also help ensure that you get to see more, and develop a greater understanding of where you are and what you are looking at. On a broader level, the following websites provide valuable background, both general and specific, on rainforests and their wildlife:

The United Nations Environment Programme's World Conservation Monitoring Centre website contains useful information a vast range of subjects, from climate change through biodiversity to individual species accounts and conservation legislation. The sections and links on mangrove forests are especially interesting (**www.unep-wcmc.org**).

Some of the rainforests in this book are listed as World Heritage Sites, and more information about them, and what WHS status means, is available at **whc.unesco.org**.

There are now more organisations dedicated to the protection and conservation of wildlife and habitats than at any point in human history, and all of them are involved with rainforests in some way. The biggest players include: Birdlife International (**www.birdlife.org**); Fauna & Flora International (**www.fauna-flora.org**); The Nature Conservancy (**www.nature.org**); The Royal Society for the Protection of Birds (Sumatra project) (**www.rspb.org.uk/supporting/campaigns/sumatra**); The Wildlife Conservation Society (**www.wcs.org**); The World Conservation Union (**www.iucn.org**); and The World Wide Fund for Nature (**www.panda.org**).

Organizations/sites with a specific emphasis on rainforests or on places included in this book include: Amazon Watch (**www.amazonwatch.org**); Ancient Forest International (temperate rainforests particularly) (**www.ancientforests.org**); Fundación de Conservación Jocotoco (Ecuador) (**www.fjocotoco.org**); Raincoast Conservation Foundation (British Columbia, Canada) (**www.raincoast.org**); The Rainforest Foundation (especially concerned with indigenous peoples of the rainforest) (**www.rainforestfoundation.org** & **www.rainforestfoundationuk.org**); Rainforest Action Network (**www.ran.org**); The Rainforest Alliance (**www.rainforest-alliance.org**); and The World Land Trust (**www.worldlandtrust.org**) (see also **www.wildlifefocus.org** and page 256).

Organizations focused more on the state of the environment *per se*, which inevitably includes campaigns and projects related to rainforests, include: Friends of the Earth (**www.foe.org**); Greenpeace (**www.greenpeace.org./international**); and People & The Planet (**www.peopleandplanet.net**).

Excellent information on the rainforests that rank among the world's top locations in terms of biodiversity can be found at **www.biodiversityhotspots.org**. The Earthwatch Institute (**www.earthwatch.org**) supports and funds scientific research into a range of habitats, including rainforests.

LEFT The Squirrel Monkey *Saimiri sciureus* is one of the commonest primates in the rainforests of the Amazon. Highly active and vocal, they move rapidly through the trees in search of food.

Glossary

Biodiversity – Biological wealth of a particular area or habitat type, usually defined as the number of species found there. Rainforests are the most biodiverse habitats on the planet.

Biomass – Total weight of all living organisms within a particular area or ecosystem. Rainforests have a greater biomass than any other habitat type.

Bushmeat – Term given to wild birds and animals that are hunted and killed for their meat. Originally targeted only by subsistence hunters, bushmeat is increasingly sold in commercial markets and even exported.

Buttress – Tree root that extends out from the trunk and helps support and stabilize the tree. Can reach heights of 4 metres (13 feet) or more.

Canopy – The uppermost layer of foliage in a forest (although see **Emergent**). Canopy heights vary according to rainforest type, but are typically 20–40 metres (65–130 feet) above the forest floor.

Cloudforest – Montane rainforest (usually above 2,000 metres/6,000 feet) that is almost constantly enveloped in mist or cloud. Particularly rich in epiphytes.

Dipterocarp – Typical lowland rainforest tree, member of Dipterocarpaceae. Over 500 species, some of which are among the tallest of all rainforest trees. Particularly well represented in Southeast Asia.

Ecosystem – Network of interacting elements, both living and non-living, within a particular area.

Elfin woodland – Vegetation type that occurs above cloudforest, characterized by the stunted nature of the trees and shrubs.

Emergent – Tree that grows higher than those around it, its crown therefore standing above the main canopy.

Endemic – Species that is restricted to a specific geographical area or habitat type. Rainforests support some of the highest rates of endemism in the world.

Epiphyte – Plant that grows on another plant but does not derive nutrition from it (and so is neither parasitic nor detrimental to its host). The most common examples in rainforests are orchids, bromeliads, ferns, mosses and lichens. Also known as air plants.

Folivore – Species of animal (or bird – such as the Hoatzin) that lives off foliage.

Frugivore – Species of animal or bird that lives primarily off fruit.

Indigenous – Native (or local) to a particular geographical area or habitat.

Mudstorey – The zone between the understorey and the main canopy layer.

Neotropical – Pertaining to the Neotropics or New World tropics of Central and northern/central South America.

Nurse log – Fallen log on which tree seedlings grow, giving rise to lines of young trees known as colonnades. Found mostly in temperate rainforests.

Pioneer – Fast-growing and light-loving species – usually plants – which rapidly colonize gaps that open up in the forest environment.

Old-growth forest – See **Primary forest**.

Podocarp – Typical rainforest tree, with almost 200 species found mainly in Australasia and South America.

Primary forest – Mature forest that has not been logged or affected by human activity in any way. Sometimes referred to as old-growth forest.

Relict – Species that previously had a wider distribution but which is now highly restricted, usually as a result of climatic or environmental change.

Riparian (Riverine) forest – Often dense and lush forest growing along the banks of rivers and other watercourses.

Secondary forest – Forest that has had its mature trees logged and thereby its canopy removed. The resulting lush regrowth, composed largely of pioneer species, may take many decades (or even longer) before it assumes old-growth characteristics.

Slash-and-burn agriculture – Form of shifting cultivation traditional in many rainforests. An area of forest vegetation is cut down and then burned, thereby clearing a plot for crop planting. The ash acts as a short-term fertilizer.

Succession – Process by which fast-growing pioneer species colonize a cleared area of forest and are in turn replaced by slower-growing but more permanent species.

Terra firme – Area of rainforest that is above a floodplain and therefore never subject to flooding.

OPPOSITE **Rainforests are the richest habitat on Earth. Birdlife is especially prolific; in parts of the Amazon it is possible to see over 350 species in just one day. This is a Long-billed Woodcreeper** *Nasica longirostris.*

Index

Page numbers in *italic* refer to illustrations.

Acknowledgements

The author is grateful to the following people for their help and advice: Jo Anderson, Miles Barber, Adam Barlow, C.A. Bashir, Gustavo Cañas-Valle, Lee Dalton, Chris Darimont, Elisabeth Fahrni Mansur, Charles Francis, Chris Genovali, Christina Greenwood, Tim Harris, Andrés Hernández-Salazar, Isobel Hunter, Luke Hunter, Michele Menegon, Xavier Muñoz, Fran Nichols, Simon Papps, Mercedes Rivadeneira, Francesco Rovero, Nigel Simpson, Hashim Tyabji, Malcolm and Sue Whittley, Thomas Zachariah and his colleagues at Kalypso Adventures.

Particular thanks go to project editor Gareth Jones, for his good humour and stoical patience throughout, to Gülen Shevki-Taylor for her creative art direction, to Liz Dittner for her insightful editorial hand, to Steve Behan for picture research, and to Emma Wicks and Anna Pow for their work on design.

Picture Credits

The World Land Trust

The World Land Trust has been saving threatened tropical forests, acre by acre, for nearly 20 years. Launched in 1989, originally to save forests in Belize which were on the verge of being logged, the Trust has gone on to save approximately 152,000 hectares (375,000 acres) of tropical forests, and other critically threatened habitats, which would otherwise have been lost forever.

The WLT is fortunate to include among its supporters some of the planet's best-known conservationists, zoologists and botanists, and we have been able to form partnerships with over a dozen like-minded organizations all over the world. Our mission is to work through overseas non-governmental partners to purchase and protect land to save habitats and their biodiversity. The land is bought from private owners, with clear undisputed title, which the WLT vests in the local organisation, and works with them to ensure long-term conservation and legal protection for the land. The WLT has provided the funds that have helped save more than 200,000 hectares (500,000 acres) of threatened habitats. We have helped save nearly five per cent of the forests of Belize, the first nature reserve in the coastal steppes of Patagonia, vast areas of Dry Chaco in Paraguay, Atlantic rainforests in Brazil, as well as a coral-fringed island in the Philippines, and corridors for elephants in India.

Urgent land purchase and protection projects are currently saving habitats in Argentina, Brazil, Ecuador, Paraguay, India and Mexico, and past projects have successfully created private nature reserves in Belize, Costa Rica, Patagonia and the Philippines. Habitats being saved are all unique and, where possible, they are connected to existing protected areas to safeguard species that migrate both altitudinally and latitudinally. In many cases the reserve areas are chosen to protect a flagship species: for instance, the first reserve in Ecuador was created to save the tiny range of the Jocotoco Antpitta *Grallaria ridgelyi*, a bird which was only discovered in 1997. The Tapichalaca Reserve now covers 4,000 hectares (10,000 acres) and, as well as protecting the Jocotoco Antpitta, it also protects tanagers and hummingbirds, over 100 Red Data Book plant species and a dozen globally endangered frog species. Spectacled Bear *Tremarctos ornatus* and Woolly Mountain Tapir *Tapirus pinchaque* also occur on the reserve. It is a similar story in India, where the elephant corridors, protecting traditional migratory routes between forest reserves, are protecting not only the Asiatic Elephant *Elephas maximus*, but also a wide variety of other wildlife including Clouded Leopard *Neofelis nebulosa*, Tiger *Panthera tigris*, and many species of deer and monkeys. This means that wider biodiversity is being protected via flagship species.

The WLT is also doing its bit for the fight against climate change by offering companies and individuals an opportunity to offset their carbon emissions by growing and preserving forests that "lock up" carbon dioxide. This works alongside land purchase projects, as land that has been cleared to make way for agriculture and other development in the past can be purchased and reforested to add to existing reserves to create larger habitats for wildlife to live and move safely. Another WLT initiative is putting webcams in the rainforest to keep an eye on the many endangered species, using the internet as a tool for conservation. At the moment a webcam in the Buenaventura Reserve in southern Ecuador is streaming live footage of a hummingbird feeder in an area where, so far, 32 species of hummingbird have been recorded. The trust also hopes the camera can show the mammal species that live in the reserve, such as Pumas *Puma concolor*, Ocelots *Leopardus pardalis*, Peccaries *Tayassuidae*, Howler Monkeys *Alouatta* sp., Spectacled Bear and Tapir *Tapirus* sp., as well as bats, reptiles and flora (see www.wildlifefocus.org for more information).

It costs £50 to purchase and protect an acre of land through the WLT. These are real acres in real places and you can even visit them, staying in low-impact nature lodges in Ecuador, Brazil and Paraguay. If you aren't able to make a trip to South America it will soon be possible to make "virtual visits" via the Trust's website — the next best thing, and certainly more environmentally-friendly than making the journey.

Climate change, forest loss, endangered species are all huge issues, about which we often feel helpless, but saving acres, hectares, square kilometres, can all represent a very positive solution to the problems facing the world's natural environments, and in addition the strengthening of local NGOs is an equally important way forward.

Registered charity 1001291
Patrons: Sir David Attenborough, OM CH FRS and David Gower, OBE